HOW TO
WRITE A WILL
AND
GAIN PROBATE

HOW TO WRITE A WILL AND GAIN PROBATE

Marlene Garsia

KOGAN
PAGE

First published in Great Britain in 1989 by
Kogan Page Limited, 120 Pentonville Road,
London N1 9JN.

While every care has been taken to ensure the accuracy
of the contents of this work, no responsibility for loss
occasioned to any person acting or refraining from
action as a result of any statement in it can be
accepted.

British Library Cataloguing in Publication Data

Garsia, Marlene
　How to write a will and gain probate.
　1. England. Wills. Composition. Amateurs' manuals
　I. Title
　344.2065'4

　ISBN 1-85091-959-3
　ISBN 1-85091-827-9 Pbk

Typeset by DP Photosetting, Aylesbury, Bucks
Printed and bound in Great Britain by
Biddles Ltd, Guildford

CONTENTS

ACKNOWLEDGEMENTS

I would like to thank all those who have helped me in writing this book. In particular Chris Marsh, Registrar, Birmingham Probate Registry; Grace Fraser, Deputy Commissary Clerk at HM Commissary Office in Edinburgh; Wykeham Garsia of solicitors Hadgkiss, Hughes and Clayton; and Ian Hills for the two chapters on taxation.

The examples in this book are based on taxation rates applicable in 1988–89.

FOREWORD

Why is it that on average only one person in four applies for probate themselves? Why do the majority of people who make a will do so through a solicitor? Two years ago some 64,000 letters of administration were issued in respect of people who had failed to make a will. So why did these people not bother to make out a will?

Could the answer be because the law is so daunting that we feel frightened to tackle even the simplest of legally based tasks and therefore have to seek professional help? Whether it is handling the conveyance of our house or writing our own will, we do not seem to trust our capabilities. Or could it be that we need information to guide us before we feel safe enough to tackle the task? I am not advocating that you will always be able to cope with your own legal problems. Some, by their very nature, do need a legal mind to sort them out, but there are instances when a DIY approach, provided it is done carefully, could be adequately carried out by an inexperienced person without involving professionals – and paying their fees too! Or lastly, do we not feel inclined to direct who should inherit our estate?

This book has been written for most people, from those who want to know but do not know whom to ask to those who still have questions, perhaps about the value of their estate. It has been written by a layperson for a layperson. And it has been written in plain English with as little use of legalistic words and phrases that the text will allow. The book is a practical and basic guide on how to write a will and gain probate. After all, it is a subject which touches all our lives at one stage or another!

In researching this book it has become clear that, under English law, provided an estate is relatively straightforward, complicated trusts are not involved, and extensive estate planning is not needed, then there is nothing to stop the individual from handling his or her own affairs – whatever the size of the estate. Despite this, only a minority of people do so. Scotland is another matter. I have explained briefly the position in Scotland, dealing with small estates, the differences when writing a will and gaining confirmation. The information given is not exhaustive since in Scotland solicitors' help is often required by the authorities. And the level of assistance is not available to the same degree as that found in England and Wales nor do matters appear as straightforward – except for processing small estates.

From the outset, I have been greatly assisted by some members of the legal profession, not to mention a member of the accountancy world. The appropriate authorities both in England and Scotland have been extremely helpful as they would be to any person seeking their assistance.

I have started at the very beginning, with what I would have to do myself when writing a will and working on from that point. Therefore this book has been written sequentially, step by step, so that readers can clearly follow what to do next whether writing their own will, planning their estate or acting as executors carrying out their obligations on behalf of a deceased friend or relative. Frequently asked questions are answered. For example, what makes a will invalid? How do you write your own will? Who can be called upon to deal with an estate? Where do you find your nearest Probate Registry? What happens if you die without making a will?

Family responsibilities necessitate family and financial decisions. How do you best ensure that your children's inheritance is not taken away by the tax inspector? What options are available when arranging your affairs? Is insurance the answer?

The readers who use this book will find it helpful in all relevant aspects, but it is not meant as a bible in which all questions are asked and answered. However, you can take heart, as you will find no unexplained text to baffle you, merely straightforward information as to what needs to be done and how to do it.

One final point: although this book mainly uses masculine pronouns throughout its contents, where appropriate, this naturally should be taken to mean both men as well as women.

= INTRODUCTION =

Everyone at some time or another find themselves faced with making arrangements following a death of a relative or close friend. At this distressing time, any mention of a will (much less the proving of it) will be seen as an intrusion into personal grief, indeed an invasion of privacy at a time when you feel least able to cope.

This book cannot help in alleviating the suffering that will be felt. What it can do is to provide information about what will be needed and what matters have to be dealt with in as straightforward and uncomplicated a manner as the subject allows. It tells you what to do and why, and how to go about it. It takes a step-by-step view on the necessary procedures from writing a will to estate planning and proving a will.

The first part of the book will be concerned with how to write a will. Basically you 'make' a will because you want to direct who receives your assets following your death. Occasionally, you may even want to ensure that certain people do not take a share. You may have already made your will either with the help of a solicitor or on a standard proprietary will form available from most large newsagents. However, if you have not done either then it is a matter that must be considered as an urgent task. If you have already made out a will, as your personal situations change then, if necessary, a new will should be written.

Examples of a basic will and specific clauses which may be added in different circumstances are also to be found. How to make an addition to your will (a codicil) is also shown.

Approximately one in every five persons writes their own will.

In London the figure is less – one in every three, while in Scotland the figure is approximately one in every four. However, most people still go to a solicitor, not because their affairs are complex but because they do not know where to start.

Estate planning and inheritance tax are also examined. For the inexperienced this subject can not only be bewildering but frightening too.

At the end of Chapter 8 the local offices of the Probate Registry in England and Wales are listed. These offices are the first place to start. For the addresses in Scotland, see Chapter 11.

Scottish law differs in many ways from the law of England and Wales. These differences are noted in one separate chapter.

Within the limitations of this book, the basic differences for both making and proving a will (and for obtaining confirmation in Scotland) are defined and clarified.

Naturally, if your affairs are complicated with, perhaps, the existence of a trust fund, an existing business or other external factors which affect the estate, then the best person to go to would be a solicitor. Solicitors are experts not only in drawing up wills but trust funds too and can act as executors of an estate. However, do be aware that these services have to be paid for. The fee was based on the value of the estate but now it refers to the length of time (and expenses too) taken to handle the affairs. Payment provision for handling probate should be noted in your will.

Banks will also advise on preparing wills and dealing with probate matters. The fee route is similar to that of solicitors. Usually banks are more expensive and have a minimum fee as well. There is a benefit in using a solicitor: you do have an authority to refer to if you think the charge is too high or the work unsatisfactory. If this happens to you then contact the Law Society and ask for its opinion.

Once a will has been made it is no use placing it in a obscure location. You should inform your executor(s) where it will be kept. Indeed, it may be prudent to leave a copy of it with your solicitor or at your bank.

If you die without leaving a will then the laws of intestacy apply to your estate. This means that your estate is divided among your surviving blood relatives according to specific rules laid down by Parliament. If there are no living relatives, once an extensive search has been undertaken, then your money goes to the Crown. This surely must be reason enough for ensuring that you make out a will!

These rules are, of course, made in broad terms and cannot take account of your individual wishes. So it is possible that a close relative who you may not have wanted to be a beneficiary will take a share of your estate. Conversely, a close friend or relative by marriage whom you may wish to benefit will not do so unless you make a will.

A White Paper is currently being circulated which examines closely the position of the surviving spouse under intestacy rules if a will has not been left. The paper looks at various ways of ensuring that a spouse can have a fairer share of the estate. Although it has suggested a number of possibilities and raised a few questions, it felt unable to recommend any particular course of action at the time of writing.

The second part of the book deals with probate. What steps should be taken and when in order to prove a will.

If the sad task of winding up the estate of a close relative or friend is placed under your agreed control, you may need to seek advice. The best place to start is at your nearest Probate Registry or at one of its sub-registries. The Registrar and his colleagues in the Personal Applications Department deal on a daily basis with all sorts of queries raised regarding probate. Of course, the State has laid down certain rules which have to be followed by them. The rules are there to protect the wishes of the deceased and to ensure that those wishes are fulfilled.

Wills can be turned down as invalid but most are accepted as having been properly made according to the laws applicable. The Registrar has some discretion in respect of what may be accepted without query but he too has rules to follow. He cannot, of course, change a will nor can he give an opinion as to its meaning other than for the specific purpose of deciding who may be entitled to be appointed to administer the estate.

If your affairs are complicated or involved then this book may not be for you. Unless you have the right legal training (or knowledge) then you may have to call upon your professional legal adviser in at least one aspect. But the fact that your estate is of considerable value does not in itself create problems. The procedure to follow is the same whether an estate has little value or great value.

In probably 95 per cent of cases a layperson is capable of dealing with his or her own affairs without any assistance from professionals. For this majority who feel capable and able to cope within constraints then this book is here as a guide.

1

WHY DO YOU NEED A WILL?

For most people the thought of making a will is depressing and because of this it is put aside for another day. Granted such a gloomy task, confirming the inevitability of your own fate, is hardly inspiring. However, sooner or later the task has to be done as it is an essential part of administering your personal affairs.

Most people own their own car, have household furniture and some even own a house. By making a will you are directing who should receive your possessions following your death. Without one you are considered to have died 'intestate' and the intestacy laws apply. In Scottish and English law if there are no traceable surviving relatives then all of your possessions, in other words 'your estate', less any debts or liabilities, go to the Crown.

The greater percentage of the population at present do not bother to make a will. How many times have you said: 'I do not have that much to leave, so why bother to make a will out?' Or, 'There is only this house and my car so it is not necessary.' Or, 'Why should it concern me as to who get what? I will, after all, not be around.' Or lastly, 'Estate planning. I won't have to pay the tax.'

The wealth of this nation has dramatically increased over the last 10 years. It is not just the privileged few who have money and assets to leave to their family and friends. The increase in house prices has been one of the most significant adjustments to personal wealth over the last decade. Even the smallest property is now valued at sums of money previously not thought possible. Add to this the value, albeit second-hand, of a car, an insurance policy, personal household effects, the odd item of jewellery, china or paintings, perhaps a few shares in a denationalised company bought after the Big Bang of 1986 and you can quite easily account for £100,000 or more. Once the current magical figure of £110,000 is attained then the tax authority reaches out for its share of your wealth. Of course, you may feel generously inclined towards the authority, but by correctly providing in your will you can lessen the amount that is demanded and which has to be paid. Whatever your argument, directly or indirectly, you – or rather your estate – has to pay the tax.

Problems can occur when writing your own will. The most frequent problem with DIY wills is that they are not worded clearly. Other errors can occur. For example, in Scotland a will, apart from the signatures of the witnesses, must also include the witnesses' full details such as names, addresses and occupations. Again, over the border in Scotland, if the will is handwritten by the testator, ie a holograph will, then witnesses are not required.

A will does not come into effect until death has occurred. A testator does not become a testator until he dies nor does an executor become an executor until this happens. So until this event the contents of a will and a will itself can be changed. If there are minor alterations then these changes can be inserted in the form of a codicil. If changes occur frequently or if they are major ones then it is better to write a new will. Remember, if a new will is drawn up then the old one should be destroyed, provided, of course, that you are satisfied that the new one has been drawn up properly and signed and witnessed correctly.

You can also include any specific arrangements you may wish to make regarding your own funeral in your will. Or perhaps you wish to donate your body to medical research or organ donation. So a will is used not only for listing who should receive what asset from your estate. Your executor should also be made aware of certain provisions in your will, namely funeral arrangements, organ donations and so on.

If there is a rule when writing your own will it must be to keep it simple. Do not stray into legal technicalities. Instead, set out what gifts are to be made, clearly identifying all objects and clearly stating who should receive them.

Who can make a will?

1. A child under the age of 18 cannot make a will.

However, if you are under the age of 18 and in Her Majesty's armed forces on active service, then you will be able to make a will which will stand as a valid one.

2. A person of unsound mind.

Obviously a person must be of sound mind and capable of managing his affairs when signing a will. However, if after making your will, through illness or an accident, you become unsound of mind then the will remains valid.

The point at which a person becomes unsound of mind can be challenged and so it is important to be able to substantiate the condition medically.

The Mental Health Act defines a person suffering from severe subnormality as one who is in a state 'of incomplete development of mind which includes sub-normality of intelligence and is of such a nature or degree that the patient is incapable of living an independent life or of guarding himself against serious exploitation or will be so incapable of an age to do so.'

Grand Uncle Herbert talking to himself in the garden or your grandmother having an invisible friend is not cause for challenging either will in court. In all probability they would not be seen as being of unsound mind but possibly suffering from a mild dose of eccentricity.

3. If a beneficiary, knowing that he was a beneficiary, murdered the testator, then the beneficiary would no longer be able to benefit from that will.

4. Since 1964, even if you hold a foreign passport but are still resident in this country, there is no distinction in law between owning property in the United Kingdom (under English law) and leaving it in your will to a person who resides abroad. Property can also be held overseas and left to someone residing in this country.

Distribution of immovable property held overseas has to be carried out in accordance with the law of the land in which that property is situated. This should serve as a reminder, when purchasing property overseas, to enquire what inheritance tax laws apply there.

Decide on your aims

Before making a will think what you want to achieve by it. Are you married? Have you any children? Are there any other beneficiaries you wish to include, such as parents, brothers, sisters, distant relatives? Are you likely to leave any money to charity? Have you considered organ donation?

Once you have considered what you want to achieve then draw up a list noting exactly what assets you have and how best

17

to distribute your estate to fulfil your wishes. Whatever you own is considered to be an asset: a car, any items of furniture, jewellery, paintings, house, securities and so on. Add to this any money you may have in savings accounts, along with details of any insurance policies or investments you hold. Literally, everything you own, from half-shares in the family silver to half-shares in an old jalopy.

Now list, in order of priority, those people you wish to benefit from your will. You may want your daughter to have all your jewellery and a friend might appreciate a specific item such as a ring, a painting or any item that holds particular fond memories. If you are married you will probably wish your children to receive the money from your life insurance policy, a share of the house, any pension rights you have, investments and so on. Alternatively, you may decide to split it, leaving some to your wife and the rest to your children. You might want the cats' home to receive a sum of money. Whatever you decide, note alongside each item whom you wish it to go to.

A will is the 'last wish' of a person and so expresses what you want to happen after your death. However, some wishes may not be actionable. For example, if you do not ask the people who you have selected to be your executors whether they are prepared to take on the task, they could well turn it down. You may wish to be buried in your local churchyard, but without prior permission from the vicar you may be put to rest in another cemetery. And if you died while living abroad, arrangements would have to be made (and finance found) to bring your body back.

Again, another example is that of guardianship. If you wish to appoint a person or persons as your children's guardians in the case of your and your spouse's death, then do ensure that you have their agreement that they are willing to take on this responsibility. Also, you will need to have a special document drawn up by your solicitor.

How much will my estate be worth in, say, 20 years' time?

How long is a piece of string? This eventuality is, however, taken care of. Your executor values your estate at the date of death. Any items not specially mentioned in your will would come under the term 'residue of estate', in other words everything you own or have legal title to. Whoever is left the residue of the estate would inherit the additional items not already disposed of. But to ensure that a relatively newly acquired specific gift goes to the right person, as your personal circumstances change so should your will. Every few years examine what you now have and, if necessary, make out a new will.

Understanding the jargon

So far in this text fairly straightforward words have been used, such as estate, beneficiary, testator, residue and so on. However, there are some less familiar words that you will come across and which will be used quite frequently from now on. The next few pages contain a glossary of terms of such words and phrases.

Absolute. Given without any condition. For example, 'I give to ... the residue of my estate absolutely' means just that. Whatever is left in the estate is given absolutely over to that named person.

Administrator. A person appointed by the Probate Registry in the absence of a will being found or a person who is appointed to prove a will in the event of there being no executor. A relative or close friend of a beneficiary could be asked to administer the estate in order of benefical priority.

Assets. Your possessions which, apart from bank accounts, insurance policies etc, include furniture, cars, jewellery – generally everything.

Beneficiary. A person who inherits (benefits) under a will or under intestacy laws or under a trust.

Bequest. A gift of estate other than immovable property (houses or land).

Bond of caution. According to Scottish law it represents a sum of money which can compensate the estate for any loss caused by an executor's mistake or omission.

Chargeable gift. An item given under the conditions of a will on which tax may have to be paid.

Children. This term now covers both legitimate and illegitimate children, also children who have been legally adopted into the family. It does not include stepchildren. Such persons must therefore be specifically mentioned if they are to benefit under a will.

Confirmation. The Scottish equivalent of a grant of probate.

Crown. This refers to the Government, whatever department.

Deceased. The person who has died.

Descendants. Any member of your blood line such as children, grandchildren and so on.

Devise and bequeath. To give a gift.

Distribution. The process of dealing with an estate after receiving the Grant of Probate or Letters of Administration, first paying debts and then dividing up the remainder between the beneficiaries.

Docket. Scottish term for a formal note.

Donee. A person who receives a gift.

Donor. A person who gives the gift.

Engrossment. Final copy of a legal document.

Executor. A person appointed by you in your will to deal with the estate. This person cannot charge a fee unless previously authorised by the will, although he or she is able to reclaim out-of-pocket expenses.

Husband. Your spouse who is still alive at the time the will is made (the same definition for Wife). In the case of divorce under English law, a couple is still legally married until the decree absolute. For Scottish law, see Chapter 11.

Infant. Now usually referred to as a Minor – in other words a person who is under the age of 18. The law at the moment states that a minor cannot legally hold possessions from an estate until the age of 18. If an asset has been given then it is given under the terms of a trust to the parent or guardian (known as trustee) for the benefit of the infant until the age of majority has been reached. You can, if you wish, declare that the minor is to take possession of the legacy before he or she attains his or her majority.

Interest. The right to your property. If total then it is called *Absolute Interest*.

Intestate. Dying without a will.

Issue. This means all living descendants.

Joint tenant. This term is applied when two or more people jointly own property. Upon the death of one of them that person's share passes to the surviving joint tenant or tenants. However, the value of the estate that is passed on to the surviving tenant(s) still has to be calculated for inheritance tax purposes. No tax is payable if the surviving joint tenant is the spouse.

Legacy. A gift of money or property other than house or land.

Legal rights. Under Scottish law this means that the surviving spouse and/or children are entitled, irrespective of the will, to benefit from the estate. Limited rights for a spouse are also now included in English law.

Life interest. The right to enjoy the benefit for life of either money or house or land or, in fact, any property. It reverts to the testator's estate upon the death of the person who enjoyed the life interest.

Life tenant. The person who benefits from a life interest.

Moveable property. This refers to any property other than land or buildings.

Next of kin. Your closest living relative.

Pecuniary legacy. A specific gift of money in your will, ie 'I give £100 to John Brown'.

Personal representative. The person appointed by the Probate Court to deal with your estate in a grant of representation. (This would include an executor named by you in your will.)

Power of appointment. The right to nominate persons to receive the benefit of a trust after your death. (Usually the person given the power is the present life tenant of the trust.)

Probate. The document issued by the Probate Court which pronounces the validity of a will and upholds the appointment of executor. In Scotland this document is known as *confirmation*.

Residue. The remainder of an estate after all legacies and bequests have been given to the donees and once all debts, taxes and expenses have been paid.

Small estate. Peculiar to Scotland, it means an estate where the gross value is less than £13,000. This should not be confused with those estates in England and Wales where, because of the small amounts of money involved ie under £5,000 and termed 'small estates', it is possible to obtain release of the monies in the estate without the legal formality of applying for a Grant.

Survivor. Any relative mentioned in the will who is still alive at the time of the testator's death. It also applies to those who may not have been born at the time the will was made, subject to limitations.

Tenant-in-common. The other way for two or more persons to hold property. In this manner each has a separate share which forms part of his estate on his death and does not automatically pass to the surviving tenant(s) in common.

Testamentary expenses. The cost of administering a will, ie expenses such as telephone, stamps, loss of wages and so on.

Testator. A person who makes a will.

Trust. Parts of an estate (or a whole estate) administered by trustees for the benefit of a named person in accordance with the trust document.

Trustee. A person nominated to deal with a trust.

2

WHAT HAPPENS IF YOU DIE WITHOUT A VALID WILL?

If you die without leaving a valid will then you are said to have died intestate. Usually in instances where one spouse dies before the other, all or the greatest share of the estate goes to the surviving spouse.

The present intestacy laws date back to 1858 when Probate Registries were first introduced. Since then they have been regularly updated to try to take account of the changes in personal circumstances and the change in the value of money.

The intestacy law, however, is now considered by some to need a complete review. The general opinion is that this law no longer adequately meets the needs for distributing the average person's estate. As the law stands, if there is a surviving spouse and issue then the spouse receives a lump sum known as the statutory legacy and half of the remaining estate for his or her life. Life interest means that the spouse cannot spend the capital of the life interest and may only use the interest obtained from investing that sum. At present the statutory legacy is £75,000 if the deceased leaves children. The value increases if there are no children, provided that the estate has the value in it.

Change in the rules governing intestacy

The Law Commission has produced a consultative White Paper aimed at examining the intestacy laws which currently exist under English law. The opinion behind the proposed change is that the surviving spouse should be better taken care of under the law. As such, the White Paper seeks to examine what route could be taken to ensure that this happens.

This 54-page document sets out to place before its readers certain recommendations, but it also states that further recommendations, not currently included in the White Paper, might be put forward for examination. At the time of writing, this paper had just been produced and any opinions at this stage are theoretical. A date for finalising these changes has not yet been given.

As changes are under way it would be worthwhile for readers to keep themselves abreast of developments.

Present rules

As the intestacy law stands now, if a person dies without a will and leaves a child, then that child will benefit from the realisation of all investments, property, etc provided he is over the age of 18. If he is not, then the share is held in trust until the child reaches the age of majority, when usually he is able to receive it. However, the trustees may, in certain circumstances, advance monies from the trust for the purpose of 'maintenance, education or advancement of the child'. When the child eventually receives the trust's estate it should include any interest earned on the money.

It cannot be stressed too often that the prime importance of making a will is that you are able to specify whom you wish to deal with your affairs and to whom you wish to leave your estate. Without a will, a government official may be appointed as administrator in certain circumstances. Any investments would then be held in a safe and cautious type of investment, not earning as great a return as possible under prevailing market conditions. By making a will and appointing an executor, one of the advantages is the flexibility allowed to that executor to move money around in a rising market in order to make the maximum profit for your heirs.

If an executor has not been appointed in a will, or if a will has not been made out, then the deceased's property – including personal belongings – will be administered by a personal representative. This representative is appointed by the Probate Registry in accordance with strict rules of priority. These rules state that a spouse has the first right to be appointed to administer the deceased's estate. But if the surviving spouse does not feel willing or able to handle the job, the couple's children may be appointed to act on their parent's behalf. When there is no surviving spouse or children then the task of administering the estate can fall on close relatives, ie parents, brothers, sisters or their issue. A close friend may be appointed attorney of the person entitled to act and, if suitable, will be appointed administrator although this does not often happen.

Whoever is appointed has a duty to adminster the estate to see that, where necessary, the assets are sold and any debts and expenses paid off. Once that has been done, distribution takes place in accordance with the Administration of Estates Act. This Act governs the distribution of an estate when the deceased has died intestate. Under the Act, if you were the appointed representative, you would have the power to deal with the estate as you thought fit in order to safeguard the assets. Of course, you are accountable for your actions.

You can claim administrative costs and out of pocket expenses from the estate, such as stamps, telephone calls and so on. Also, if you have had to forfeit a day's pay in attending to estate affairs you can reclaim the amount of pay lost.

After *letters of administration* have been granted by the Probate Registry and once all debts and expenses have been paid distribution can take place. Again, there is an order of priority.

If there is a surviving spouse he or she receives all the deceased's personal items (known as personal effects) together with a sum up to the value of the statutory legacy which is at present £75,000. Should the value of the estate exceed this, and there is also issue, then the surviving spouse would receive half of the balance of the estate for life. In other words, the half of whatever is remaining after the personal effects, the statutory legacy of £75,000, and debts and expenses have been deducted. The remaining half would go to any children immediately, except if they are under the age of 18 (see page 23).

On the death of the surviving spouse the half of the estate which he or she has had a life interest in will also pass to the children. Therefore, it is important to understand fully what *life interest* means. Life interest could be described as borrowed ownership in that you have the right to use the interest from the capital but cannot touch the capital as it does not legally belong to you. Upon death, the life interest passes to the other beneficiaries, for example, the children, and is divided up equally for their benefit.

When children are the nearest surviving relatives of the

deceased, the estate passes to them or, if some have already died leaving children of their own, to their issue, ie grandchildren or great grandchildren. The shares are held in a *Statutory Trust* for the children, in equal parts, until each reaches the age of 18 or marries, whichever happens first. The definition of children now includes legitimate, illegitimate or legally adopted children but not step children.

In a case where there is a surviving spouse but no issue, the spouse's statutory legacy increases to £120,000 in addition to the personal effects. If the estate is larger than this and there are no surviving 'issue', but other relations are alive, such as parents, brothers, sisters etc, then the spouse receives all the personal effects together with £120,000 and half of the residue of the estate absolutely, with no life interest being applicable.

If a brother or sister of the deceased dies in the deceased's lifetime, leaving children, then their children will take the deceased parent's share divided equally between them.

Should a person die leaving a surviving spouse but no children, or other issue, or indeed parents, brothers or sisters or their issue, then the surviving spouse receives the whole of the estate, irrespective of its value.

The order of inheritance of an estate where the deceased has died intestate is as follows:

1. Spouse
2. Children or other issue
3. Parents
4. Brothers and sisters of the 'whole blood' or if deceased, their issue
5. The issue of the brothers and sisters
6. Brothers and sisters of the 'half blood' (having one common parent with the deceased) and their issue
7. Grandparents
8. Uncles and aunts of the 'whole blood' and their issue
9. Uncles and aunts of the 'half blood' and their issue
10. And if there are none of the above then the estate goes to the Crown.

Often you will see a notice in the national or local papers asking for the relatives of the deceased to contact a firm of solicitors. This usually means that the administrators are trying to trace relatives of the deceased. There is a time stipulation, however. A person cannot turn up some four years after the advertisement to claim his or her inheritance; by then it will be too late.

There are three other areas surrounding intestacy under English law. First, in the case of a common law wife or husband, if a will has not been made out to include a provision for a common law wife or husband then she or he is not entitled to any part of the estate.

Second, if a marriage has ended in divorce and a decree absolute has been granted, the divorced spouse is not entitled to any part of the estate. Their children, however, will be beneficiaries. If death took place after decree nisi had been given but before decree absolute, then a spouse would still be seen in the eyes of the law to be the surviving spouse and would benefit accordingly. A spouse does not benefit if a judicial separation decree has been issued. A separation order issued by magistrates does not affect entitlement to benefit.

A divorce in England and Wales (for Scotland, see page 111) alters your will and makes any gift to your ex spouse void. However, the application of the law that creates this effect on other persons in your will may not operate as you would expect. It is very important, therefore, that a new will be made out when major events alter your life. Remember that once the new will has been written you must destroy the old one.

Lastly, when a person makes a will then later marries, in England or Wales, those parts of his or her will which refer to leaving money to the spouse will be treated as omitted or void unless it states that it is being made 'in contemplation' of that forthcoming marriage and states that the will is to remain in force after that marriage.

3

WHAT YOU SHOULD KNOW BEFORE WRITING A WILL

Anything that is fully owned by you can be left in a will. Certain assets such as those owned under a joint ownership which are already subject to an agreement to be passed on, cannot be given. Also, any property which has been left to a person under a *form of nomination* (ie National Savings Bank account) is not covered by your will even if it is referred to.

As years pass by the value of most possessions usually increases. A will written 10 or 15 years ago will be outdated as, hopefully, your possessions will have increased substantially both in quantity and value. This is why it is important to update your will by making a new one out. You may also be the beneficiary of someone else's will and may wish to name the person who, in turn, is to inherit this gift in your will. Incidentally, if you survive the donor then you, and ultimately your beneficiaries, will inherit the gift, assuming you have not disposed of it.

This does not mean rewriting your will every year but assessing every few years whether your existing will still adequately covers all your wishes and, indeed, whether your personal circumstances have changed.

What is termed as 'property'?

Whatever you own from a house to personal effects is your *property*, and forms your estate.

In addition, there is a distinction between freehold and leasehold property not only in definition but, more importantly in the context of this book, in the way it forms part of your estate. Owning the freehold of the land and buildings means it is yours for perpetuity. Leasehold property is only owned by you for as long as the leasehold tenancy. Leasehold property usually starts its life on a tenancy of 99 years. As time passes so the lease's term decreases until the expirty date.

So you can in theory leave your leasehold flat or house to your nearest relations. However, if the leasehold agreement states that you cannot assign the lease without consent of the owner of the lease, then your executor would first have to seek permission before selling the property or assigning the lease to your beneficiaries, see page 115. You can, of course, write to the lease owners and ask them to sell the lease to you at any time but only have the automatic legal right of purchase if you have lived there for four years or more.

Another direction that you can include in your will is with regard to the disposal of your body. You may wish to give particular directions for your funeral or even for what you want to have done with your body. Today it is becoming increasingly popular to carry donor cards. These cards authorise the use of various organs in your body for transplant purposes. The organs are removed shortly after death once the donor card(s) has been passed on to the doctor or subject to your nearest of kin's agreement. The next of kin can also give authorisation for removal of organs once a patient has been pronounced dead.

Financial matters

INSURANCE POLICIES

There are three main types of insurance policy that will pay out on death. First there is a *life policy* which, upon proof that death has occurred, will pay out the insured amount absolutely.

There is a further type of term insurance called the *family income benefit*. While a standard life insurance would pay out a fixed lump sum upon proof of death, family income benefit, acting as a replacement wage, would pay out each and every year through-out its term. There is an added benefit in that the amount can be made inflation proof.

This policy is not only applicable to men but should be considered by women as well. More and more women are wage earners but a fair proportion still remain at home looking after their children. Should a 'stay at home' mother die, how will the husband afford to hire a live-in nanny to care for their children? The cost of a nanny varies from north to south but on average you would pay £3500 to £10,000 a year, plus national insurance contributions.

The family income benefit's term is based on the youngest member of the family. So if you have three children ranging in age from 3 to 15, the policy would pay out for 15 years until the youngest child reached the age of 18.

There is a minus side. If the policy's period of time is 12 years and you die 6 months into that term, then your family benefit. However, if you die 11 years and 6 months into a 12-year policy, your family will only receive the remaining portion of time, namely 6 months. You can hedge your bets, however, by taking out a level-term policy which would pay out the same amount irrespective of whether you died 6 months or 6 years after the policy came into force.

Second, there is the *endowment policy*. Although it is not a life policy it usually has a life element written in. For example, you take out an endowment policy for a lump sum to be paid to you in, say, 10, 15 or 20 years' time and pay a monthly premium to the insurance company. That policy will, in most cases, have a death clause which says that if death occurs before the policy term has been completed a specifically stated sum of money will be paid out.

Last, there is a *pensions policy* which again, like the endowment policy, usually contains a death clause paying out during the term of the policy upon death.

To realise money from an insurance policy, you first have to produce the death certificate along with the policy documents and, provided you are the beneficiary of that policy and can prove this, the money will be released. Before sending all these documents off, do telephone the insurance company's head office asking for their specific requirements: and do remember to keep photocopies of all documents sent.

Inheritance tax has to be paid before probate is granted, though payment of the tax due on a house or land or any interest held in a private firm can be deferred for up to six months from the end of the month in which death took place. The tax on this part of the estate may also be paid by instalments.

If you feel that either you (if you are the beneficiary of a will) or your close relatives (beneficiaries of your will) are not able to meet the immediate charge of inheritance tax, you can take out a life policy provided you have an *insurable interest*. For example, a husband can take out this policy on his wife's life or she on his because a husband or his wife has an 'insurable interest'. If you are a single person and your brother, sister or parent was the sole beneficiary of your will then that person would also be able to take out a policy on your life.

In life insurance, *term insurance* is the cheapest and it is best to shop around to find the best deal for you. Incidentally, the premium paid by women is less as they are considered to live longer.

Whole of life is a more expensive life insurance as it guarantees a lump sum of money without stipulating a qualifying period. It also comes with a bonus option. Again, shop round for the deal most suited to your needs.

MONEY
The definition of money in a will is taken to mean all cash held, including your loose cash, whether in a purse or wallet or hidden under the bed. It also extends to a range of cash investment accounts, depending upon the context in which the will is written. These accounts range from National Savings accounts to bank and building society accounts and premium bonds. Gifts of money are termed *pecuniary legacies*.

SHARES, UNIT TRUSTS, PERSONAL EQUITY PLANS (PEPs)
As the investment markets introduce new types of investment products, so these new investments may be bought by you and in turn find their way into your will. Shares, unit trusts, PEPs can be disposed of just as if they were any other type of property given within the scope of your will. Share dividends sent after the owner's death also form part of the estate.

These assets will have to be priced at the value as of the date of death. This subject is dealt with in detail in Chapter 10, Valuing and Administering the Estate.

What is an executor? Who can be appointed?

An executor is a person who is named by you in your will to see that your wishes are carried out in accordance with the will, collect in the estate, pay any debts or expenses and then distribute the remainder to the named beneficiaries. Executors' duties only commence once death has occurred and these duties cease once the estate has been distributed to the named beneficiaries.

You should always appoint someone to be the executor of your will. Before naming that person in your will it is best to ask him or her if he or she is willing to take on the duty. It is useful but not essential to appoint someone who has had previous business experience. Whoever is appointed, he or she is obliged to carry out your exact wishes.

You may name as many executors as you wish but only four may be appointed to act by the Probate Registry at any one time. It is useful, though not essential, to name more than one person so that if one decides not to act then there will still be someone else already appointed and familiar with your wishes. If only one executor is appointed and then turns down this role the Probate Registry will apply the various rules and regulations to decide who should act in his or her place.

You can appoint a close friend or relative or a firm of solicitors, accountants or your bank to be the executor of your will. A minor or a person of unsound mind will not be allowed to act. Do be aware that if professionals agree to act then a fee will be charged. This fact will have to be written into the will stating that fees and expenses will be paid by the estate. Unless specified, a non-professional executor cannot charge a fee. There is nothing to prevent an executor from receiving a gift under the provisions laid out in the will but this gift will be seen to have been made on condition that he acts as executor, unless you state otherwise.

A private individual who acts as an executor and incurs expenses in carrying out those duties can claim back these expenses from the estate. However, he is not allowed to charge for his time in carrying out these duties. If, in his official capacity, he takes time off work and as a result loses money then he is able to reclaim this loss from the estate as part of the administration expenses.

If you have been appointed an executor but feel, for whatever reason, after the death that you cannot act then you may renounce your executorship. You would be asked to sign a *form of renunciation* either by the Probate Registry or by the solicitor acting for other persons named in the will. Should you be holding the will but for some reason are unable to pass the document on to another interested person then you may file the will at your nearest Probate Registry, signing a form stating that you do not, for whatever reason, wish to deal with the will. The Probate

Registry will then appoint a personal representative, usually the chief beneficiary of the will. The person appointed is known as the administrator.

Where should a will be kept?

There is no legal obligation to register a will in any official office. This applies wherever you live in the United Kingdom. It is up to you to keep your will in a secure place and to inform your executors or your nearest relatives of its location. If it is in a safe at home then let the executor know the combination. If it is locked in a drawer then let him have a key. Should you chose your solicitor or your bank to be one of the executors than they will usually keep the will in their safe for you.

Wills can be deposited for safekeeping with the record keeper at Somerset House. You may do this through your local Probate Registry or by calling at or writing to the Principal Registrar, Family Division, Somerset House, Strand, London WC2R 1LP. If you write, a large envelope with instructions will be sent to you. All details asked for have to be noted and it has to be signed and witnessed before being returned. Once Somerset House is in receipt of your will they will send you a deposit certificate. If you present the will personally they will hand the certificate over at that time. This certificate has to be produced by your executors after your death before the will is released to them.

The fee for keeping a will at Somerset House is nominal, ie £1. There are obvious advantages of doing it this way in that your executors know where the will is and you can rest assured that it is in one of the safest places. The draw back is that should you wish to add a codicil to your will or make out a new one, you will have to produce the certificate before withdrawing the original will. The whole procedure will have to be gone through once again and a second fee of £1 charged.

What is a trust?

It is not within the scope of this book to deal with the setting up of a trust, therefore the next few paragraphs are only a brief description.

If a trust is to be formed then you should ask a solicitor to draw one up. Remember that if a trust or life interest is to be included in a will the costs to administer it can be expensive.

A trust is formed if the deceased feels that the beneficiaries would be better catered for by one; or if the beneficiaries are under the age of majority and their needs both present and future need careful administration; for tax reasons; or because the deceased feels that his estate should be passed on in perpetuity.

By creating a trust you place your estate (or part of it) in the hands of a person who is called a *trustee*. This person is appointed to a position of trust (hence the name) to carry out the provisions as expressed in the trust.

Before making the trust, ask the person whether he wishes to be a trustee. It is best to select at least two people to become trustees.

Trustees are legally bound to deal with the trust and its assets properly and to ensure that any beneficiary of the trust receives what is rightfully due.

As in the case of executorship, a trustee does not receive a specific payment for his time unless the trust stipulates to the contrary. Of course, expenses can be reclaimed from the trust. Naturally, professionals, whether they are banks, solicitors or accountants, will charge for their time and so you must be aware of what cost is likely to be incurred before creating the trust document.

There are a few points which you should be aware of if you are setting up a trust.

1. You cannot compel a person to act as a trustee.
2. A full inventory of the trust's property must be made at the outset.
3. If there is a life interest it should state this fact in the trust and ensure that it gives the trustees power to look after whatever is included in the life interest, whether it is money, property, paintings etc.
4. The trustees are legally bound to carry out the duty specified in the trust within the laws of the land.
5. Trustees are accountable for any neglect or default throughout the administration of the estate.

Small estates in England and Wales

Not to be confused with the definition applied in Scotland (see page 104), in England and Wales estates totalling £5000 or less are considered to be small estates and a grant of probate or letters of administration are not necessary.

Some institutions, such as banks, building societies and insurance companies, state that they do not need a grant and that they can release the monies held once a release form has been drawn up. But be careful, for it is not as simple – or as cheap – as it first appears. First, there is a charge levied for this, usually a minimum of £30, and second, a fee per asset is charged for a release document.

On the other hand, to obtain a grant from the Probate Registry a fee of £5 is charged for estates of £5000. While a release document is needed for each asset held by the various banks and insurance companies, only one grant of probate or letters of administration is needed.

If, however, you do decide to use the service offered by these institutions you will have to make a declaration on the release form, usually before a solicitor or magistrate; this has to be done each time you complete one of the forms. Again, a charge is levied. In addition, it is often necessary for all benefiting persons to sign the release document, whereas if done through the Probate Registry only one or possibly two persons need to be involved with the procedure.

What is life interest?

Before making a will out you would need to decide whether you leave your house to your wife (husband) in a life interest or whether you leave it to her (him) absolutely – in other words, without any conditions. If you decide on applying life interest to the property then she would benefit from its use for the rest of her life, passing it on to other stated beneficiaries under the terms of your will upon her death. Life interest means that your spouse could live in or rent the property for the rest of her life but would not actually own it. House repairs and maintenance would obviously need to be carried out at some time, so it would have to be decided whether the life interest beneficiary would pay for this or whether it would be paid for jointly by all the beneficiaries concerned. Rentals earned would go directly to the person who is benefiting from the life interest. Whatever you decide upon, write your decision into your will.

If the life interest involves money, your spouse would receive the interest that the capital sum earned but the capital would remain intact for the other beneficiaries upon her death. For stocks and shares, the life interest would entitle her to the receipt of income (interest and dividends) but not the actual capital invested.

The benefit of life interest is that your surviving spouse has the house and income for life and the children benefit thereafter. You direct who receives what, but there is a minus side to it. First, your personal representative is not able to finalise the administration of the estate, and second, life interest can be expensive to administer. Income tax forms, trust accounts and so on will have to be completed and perhaps a financial adviser brought in too. All these experts would charge fees for handling matters. So unless your estate is of sufficient size to warrant it, or if you feel your children's rights should be safeguarded above everything in case your spouse remarries, then life interest should not be considered.

Absolute gift is simpler as it means leaving outright any possession you direct without stipulation to the named beneficiary. In fact this alternative is the more common – and cheaper – of the two.

4

WHAT CAN AFFECT YOUR WILL?

There are three ways in which your will can be revoked or made inoperable. The first two are deliberate acts through choice. You can destroy your will or you can make a new will which includes a statement that you wish to revoke the earlier document. The third one applies in England and Wales; if you get married and do not specifically state in your will that after this event you wish your current will to remain in force, your marriage would invalidate the will.

Marriage

Let us take the unconscious act of invalidating a will, that is through marriage. Scottish readers should see page 111 for the application of Scottish law. In England and Wales, to avoid invalidating your will by marriage, you can insert a statement of its intent, known as the *power of appointment* clause. By doing this, even if you marry or re-marry and the will is revoked, the clause exercising the power of appointment would still be operational. So if you expect to marry a particular person at the time the will is made out, then provided the following clause is inserted, any such will still remains valid. But remember, you must name the person you intend to marry.

EXAMPLE
'I [name] make this will in contemplation of my marriage to [name] and wish this will to remain in force after the said marriage.'

Divorce

If you apply for a divorce, upon gaining the decree absolute your former husband or wife will no longer benefit from your will and any gift made to them will be void. Unless you have made alternative provisions in your will to cover this eventuality the subject of the void gift will be dealt with as if you had died intestate. If your children are to be the stated beneficiaries then they will inherit the estate absolutely. It may be that your ex-partner will administer the estate – in the role of guardian – on your children's behalf, depending upon the terms of the divorce.

Revocation of a will

The making of a new will usually revokes a previous one provided a statement to this effect is placed in the will, namely, 'I revoke all former wills and testamentary dispositions previously made by me.' Even if this statement is included there will be an implied revocation of earlier wills if the later document clearly disposes of the whole estate.

Another instance where a will is naturally revoked is if it is deliberately destroyed by the person who has written it with the deliberate intention of revoking it. A will can also be destroyed by another person on the instructions of the testator but this must be done in his presence under his direction. If this happens the testator must categorically state to the attending person(s) that it is his intention to destroy the will and then instruct the third person to do this on his behalf.

Writing across the top of your will 'I revoke this will' does not mean that the will ceases to exist. You can, of course, accidentally destroy a will by destroying your own signature or that of your witnesses but unless the intention was there to revoke the will, legally it will still be valid.

If a codicil accompanies a will which you later revoke by destruction, unless you also destroy the accompanying codicil it will still remain in force.

Legally, you cannot unintentionally destroy your will. If you lose your will while moving house, the will is still considered to be legally in force and only by making out a new will revoking its predecessor will the old one be made void.

An example of assumed destruction of a will is if your executors cannot find your will after your death although it is known that one had been made. If it was last known to have been in your possession then there is a legal presumption that it has been revoked by you. This presumption can be rebutted by evidence showing that there was definitely no intention to revoke the will.

A 'wish of intent'

To the best of human endeavours, the State intends that the persons named in your will should benefit from your property, according to the terms of your will. However, if the language of the will is ambiguous then further investigation by the executor or, in some instances, the court may be called for. Evidence would have to be shown in order to try to interpret your wishes. This evidence can take the form of letters sent to your next of kin or conversations held with them when you expressed a 'wish of intent'. They would have to swear that this was exactly what happened, however. Any falsification of evidence would be a serious matter indeed. This is why it is so important to express clearly in your will what your intentions are.

Disputes and unknown factors

Suppose Great Uncle Harry dies without any issue, leaving you as his only descendant. If you had an argument and he decided not to leave you a legacy then, under the Inheritance (Provision for Family and Dependance) Act 1975, you are able to apply to the court to be given part of Great Uncle Harry's estate. However, you would first have to establish that you were in some way a dependant of his. The court's powers are wide and in order to stand a chance of receiving any inheritance under the Act's provisions you would have to show that you were materially supported by him, for example, he let you live under his roof, gave you food and made sure that you were physically well cared for.

A further example of unknown factors overturning the wishes of a will is if you divorced and later married a divorcee who had a child. Then if you and your new wife in turn had a child and by some misfortune you forgot to name either in your will then they would be able to put a claim in against your estate as they could be seen to be 'children of the family' and therefore dependants. Again, it is up to the discretion of the court to decide on the proportion of the estate, if any, to be paid out.

Another common wish inserted in wills which can cause

disputes is one of continuous family inheritance. It has a moral implication rather than a legal one because of the Statute of Limitations, which means life plus 70 years. Also, you cannot dictate what another person does with his or her will. In cases such as this, you can make a gift a life interest only to be passed back to the estate upon death and then on to next stated beneficiary.

Although it would not make your will invalid if you state in it that you wish your eldest child to have a certain item and in turn he or she is instructed to pass this item on to his or her eldest child it might not occur. So despite the fact that they are under a moral duty to do this, there is no legal obligation.

You cannot stipulate in your will that your house must be lived in by your son if it inflicts separation between parent and child or instigates the intention of breaking up a marriage. Such clauses are deemed to be 'contrary to public policy' and the law ensures that such stipulations do not stand. The same applies to religion. You cannot stipulate in your will that your grandchildren (or any other person) be brought up in a particular religious faith in order to inherit from your estate. To insert a clause stating that a child will be excluded from a legacy if he is brought up in a religion other than his own would be to invalidate that section of your will. Again, it is seen as contrary to public policy. The definition of a specific religion is also seen as too vague and extensive clarification would be needed.

The term 'contrary to public policy' can be seen in many different ways and nowadays will often be discarded because the phrase itself is too vague. It is supposed to reflect what is believed to be public policy at the present time.

Courts can, once petitioned, examine the disposition of gifts within the will if those gifts are regarded as contrary to public policy. However, in such instances it is up to the court on the day to decide on the individual merit of each case. Therefore, it is not possible to expand further within the terms of this book. A solicitor should be consulted where such a situation arises.

Making a gift void

Wills may be declared invalid if it is proved that they were made as a result of excessive pestering, in other words if someone tried to persuade you to leave everything you own (or even a specific gift) to them. So, if a person has imposed undue influence on you, and this can be proved, the will can be seen as invalid.

If a murder was committed by a beneficiary of a will (or indeed the beneficiary aided and abetted somebody in causing the death of the testator) then, regardless of the benefits noted in the will the murderer or accomplice would receive no inheritance. In committing the crime he or she automatically forfeits his or her right to inherit. Incidentally, it is also possible that a person found guilty of manslaughter in a motor accident which caused the death of the testator, who under the terms of the deceased's will was left an inheritance, could forfeit his legacy.

You can also invalidate a gift in your will if you, as a condition of your will, ask a beneficiary to commit an unlawful act of whatever nature. Of course, whether this is a statement in a will or not, the request is illegal.

You should not ask a beneficiary or the spouse of a beneficiary to witness your will because in so doing you are making the gift void.

Overall, it should be remembered that generally, unless a person has a valid claim, the courts do not as a rule turn aside the testator's wishes. The invalidation of your will, therefore, is not a matter which should worry you unduly.

Rules to follow

To ensure that you make a valid will there are a few rules to follow. First, you must be over 18 years of age and second, you must sign the will in the presence of two witnesses both of whom must be present at the same time. Those witnesses must then, before leaving your presence, sign their names at the bottom of the document. There is another requirement. You must also be mentally capable of understanding your actions and know what you are doing, and intending to do, when signing your will.

There is an exception to the age requirement noted above. A person over 14 but under 18 can make a will, provided that the person is on active military service in times of war. Similarly, seamen at sea in peacetime may also exercise this privilege.

It cannot be stressed too often that a will must clearly state your intentions, in other words exactly who is to receive precisely what. Many a confusion occurs and many a will is made invalid because the instructions are not clear.

'All my property' means just that – absolutely everything you own. You might have wanted the house to go to your wife and perhaps some of your personal effect; also, you may have wanted a few mementos to go to your son, mother or friend. With the use of the above phrase, they would receive nothing.

Another stumbling block when a will is being written by a layperson is the over-indulgent use of what is considered to be legal phrases. Again, you may think you meant one thing but, in fact, it would be judged as something entirely different. For example, 'I leave all monies' means, 'I leave you all my cash', Nothing else, just cash in its physical form and in bank and building society accounts. It does not include the value of the house, furnishings or any other valuable you own or, indeed, even the value that any such items could realise. Keep the phrases simple and specific, and select your words carefully.

The main tasks of the Probate Registry are to decide on the validity of a will and to interpret it for the purpose of deciding who to appoint as personal representatives. Unclear statements can cause problems when it comes to making this interpretation. In 1988 the Non-Contentious Probate Rules were introduced giving the Registrar some discretion as to enquiries which could be made with regard to establishing the validity of a will. This book cannot possibly cover all these considerations, so you should check to make sure that your will has been worded correctly.

Basically, the Registrar cannot alter the distribution arrangements as laid out in the will, although if it becomes clear that there has been some mistake in the wording because of a misunderstanding he may, on behalf of the testator, put the mistake right provided all persons affected by this action agree to it. However, the will's intentions cannot be altered so if monies are given then all cash is inherited; if a house is given then the property is passed on; and if 'all that I own' is given then everything the deceased owned must be passed on. Of course, if a wife, son or daughter or, indeed, any person who claims to be a dependant, is excluded then they can apply to the court and ask to be awarded part of the estate.

A will is accepted as valid in England and Wales without query if it appears to be signed properly and has a clause called an *attestation clause* inserted in it. (Printed wills obtained from stationers have this clause.) This clause confirms that the necessary rules have been followed when a person signs the will. If it has not been inserted, enquiries will usually have to be made to confirm that the will was properly signed.

In England and Wales an unsigned will is invalid but in Scotland (see Chapter 11) a holograph (written in the person's own hand) will is not necessarily invalid because it is not signed. Alteration made to a will after it has been properly signed will also invalidate it, unless the will is signed and witnessed again. Sometimes minor alterations do occur and provided that this happens before the will is signed, the incorrect word or line should be crossed out and the substitute one written above it. At the time the will is signed and witnessed you should place your initials alongside the altered text. The witnesses must also place their initials alongside the alterations.

The best rule to follow, however, should be that if alterations are necessary then make out a new will. Only minor alterations should be inserted in the form of a codicil. A codicil acts as an insertion in your will; for example, the amended distribution of a particular item.

It does not matter what your will has been written on provided that the Registrar sees that it is a fair copy. Registrars are used to receiving all manner of wills, from those written on brown paper to, on occasions, those presented having been written on tracing paper – although such a presentation is not recommended.

5

HOW TO WRITE A WILL

One of the greatest problems facing the Probate Registry is unclear meaning in the wording in many 'home-made' wills. While there is sufficient leeway for the Registrar to make an interpretation, in some cases this is not possible and the will then has to have its meaning defined in accordance with the rules, possibly in a higher court, namely the Chancery Court. The courts try to decipher what the deceased may have wanted to say, but a precise interpretation may not be possible because of the unclear wording. So you must state clearly, using full names, who is to receive the gift as well as giving a full description of the item or items named. For example, if you have two antique button-back chairs and you want your favourite niece to receive one then describe the chair precisely. Give the colour of the upholstery, trim and any small detail that can help in identifying the chair, and your niece's full name and current or last known address.

Checklist for your will

On a separate sheet of paper you should note what assets you have and whom you wish to benefit. When looking at the valuation of your estate, see the checklist example on page 44, make sure that it is not going to attract more inheritance tax than at first anticipated. If it is, you should take steps to examine how this liability can be lessened, see Chapters 6 and 7.

You will need to state in your will whether your individual beneficiaries have to pay inheritance tax from their legacy or whether you wish all legacies to be paid in full and any tax due to be taken out of the balance of the residue of the estate. If you have any outstanding debts, perhaps a loan from the bank or a mortgage, then this should also be noted in your lists so that these debts can be settled from the estate and the amount deducted from its total. Remember, whatever route you decide to take tax usually has to be paid before probate is granted. A loan can be obtained from a bank to raise the tax money and the interest from the loan can be deducted from the estate's value when calculating the total inheritance tax liability. However, although this route speeds up the process in that the grant may be obtained quickly, it is not the best route to take as the interest still has to be paid and although deducted from tax due, is not 100 per cent relievable, ie you still pay 60 per cent in the pound. Another route for payment of tax is if the estate holds any National Savings monies or premium bonds; then the Probate Registry can organise with these authorities for tax to be taken from such holdings.

A checklist of assets should now be drafted. For a more comprehensive list of items for inclusion see the Estate Checklist in Chapter 11, pages 107-8.

CHECKLIST OF ASSETS
EXAMPLE

Item			Amount £
House	value	£100,000	
	less mortgage	£40,000	60,000
Life insurance with [name] Co Ltd			
	on death worth		60,000
Pension with [name] Co Ltd			
	on death worth		40,000
Current value of shares and unit trusts held			5,000
Building society accounts			
	[name] Building Society (1)		1,500
	[name] Building Society (2)		1,900
Bank accounts with [name]			
	current		750
	deposit		5000
Second-hand value of car			2,500
Half of furnishing and personal effects			5,000
Approximate total			£181,650

EXAMPLE: Notes for legacy in, [name], will

1. My wife, [name], is to have the house, car, money in the building society and bank accounts, furnishings except for those listed below, half the proceeds of my life insurance policy with [insurance company's name] and the residue of my estate.
2. My children, [name] and [name], to receive half of the proceeds from my pensions policy with [insurance company's name], half the proceeds of my life insurance with [insurance company' name] to be held in trust with my wife as trustee.
3. To my brother, [name], half of the value of my shares and unit trusts and my Hornby train set.
4 To my mother, [name], half of the value of my shares and unit trusts and my gold fob watch with chain.
5 To my friends, [name] and [name], the gate-legged oak card table with red leather top.
6. If my wife dies before me, ask my brother, [name], to set up a trust and act on the children's behalf.

In this example, the estate is valued at over £110,000 so estate planning would be needed to see if there were any ways in which the estate's tax liability could be reduced.

Before moving on to the writing of a will and different examples of clauses which can be inserted, it is worth noting that you are able to purchase a printed will form from any of the large high street stationers. However, there is not a great deal of space allowed for the provision of various legacies and additional sheets would have to be inserted.

When writing your own will there is one clause which must always be included. Many a new will is written and the old one is forgotten or ignored. The phrase which should be inserted in every new will is, 'I revoke all former wills and codicils and testamentary provisions.' If you make a new will forgetting to destroy the earlier one, and if this *revocation clause* is not included, then the latter will may not prevail in its entirety. On occasions when this happens both documents have been proved and the combined provisions, provided they are not inconsistent with each other, are applied.

Always keep a carbon copy or a photocopy of your will whether it is handwritten or typed.

The following checklist of sentences appear in sequence in any will. The letters at the start of each sentence refer to the example of a will to be found on pages 47–9 and to further inclusions which are found on pages 49–51.

(A) A will should always start with the sentence 'This is the last will and testament of [name]'.

(B) This statement is followed by your full name, your full current address and the date that the will is being made.

(C) A statement revoking all previous wills and codicils and testamentary provisions is inserted next.

(D) A statement appointing your executors and noting whether any payment is to be made to them.

(E) If you have any particular wishes, such as funeral arrangements, then these wishes should be inserted next.

(F) A statement that all estate expenses incurred (known as *testamentary expenses*) should be paid by the estate. Also this section should state whether the gifts made in the will are to be free of inheritance tax liability. If this is the case then you will have to allow for the correct amount when first preparing your estate valuation.

(G) Now you list any specific gifts of money (known as *pecuniary legacies*) in detail, stating who is to receive what amount. The following statement should be made for each gift. 'I give and bequeath the following legacy to [name] of [address] ...'.

(H) Under (G), the following statement listing other legacies is inserted for each gift. 'I give and bequeath the following to [name] of [address] ...'. Note carefully what gift is to be received and if it is, say, a house or a piece of land then note the exact location.

(I) You should end your will with a clause disposing of those assets which you have not as yet given to anyone. The *residue* or remainder of the estate would go to this person once all debts (inheritance tax, funeral expenses and so on) have been paid. A suitable clause would be; 'I devise and bequeath the residue of my real and personal estate [name] of [address] ...'.

In addition, a *survivorship clause* is inserted stating that should this main beneficiary not survive you by 30 days then the residue of the estate should go to another named person. This is done to clarify any possible claim by beneficiaries from either side should, for example, both husband and wife die in the same accident where the precise time of death could not be established. If the husband died in an accident and 10 days later his main beneficiary, ie his wife, also died, then the residue of his estate which was being left to her would to his other chief beneficiary. Without this clause the husband's estate would have been given across to his wife's estate for distribution according to the bequests of her will.

(J) This statement is followed by what is known as the *attestation clause*. 'Signed by the said testator in the presence of us, present at the same time and by us in his presence.' Here you sign your name and the signatures of your two witnesses also appear here, below your signature. Each witness must also write his full current address. (Note: neither a spouse nor a beneficiary of the will may witness the will. The spouse of a beneficiary must also not witness the will, otherwise the gift is forfeit.)

As individual needs and circumstances differ so each will and its content will reflect these differences. A married man with a wife and child will want to ensure that they were well provided for. An elderly person who has no close relatives would perhaps want to leave her estate not only to relatives but to charity or friends. A single person with perhaps a brother or sister, will have different priorities and the same would apply to a widow or widower. The sample will that follows allows for the adoption of different clauses which different people may want to include. The letters in brackets relate to the previous list of statements which should appear in a will.

Example of a will

(A) THIS IS THE LAST WILL AND TESTAMENT OF (B) Edith Mary Baker of Broadwood, Non-Such Lane, Burton, Warwickshire made this seventh day of October one thousand nine-hundred and eighty-eight.

(C) I hereby revoke all former wills codicils or other testamentary provisions at any time made by me and declare this to be my last will.

(D) I appoint my husband, James Arthur Baker of Broadwood, Non-Such Lane, Burton, Warwickshire and my son Richard John Baker of Rose Cottage, Hill Street, Minford and Mr J Blogham of J Blogham and Sons, High Street, Minford, Warwickshire to be the executors of my will and Mr J Blogham shall be entitled to charge and to be paid for all professional or any other charges for any business or acts done by him in connection with this will.

(E) I express the wish that my body be buried in the graveyard at Burton Church.

(F) All gifts are subject to the payment of my just debts, funeral and testamentary expenses and all taxes and duties payable.

(G) I devise and bequeath to each of my grandchildren who shall be living at the time of my death the sum of £2000.

I give and bequeath the sum of £2000 to the Burton Dogs Home, Mile End Lane, Burton, Warwickshire.

(H) I give and bequeath my freehold land and property of Somerset Farm, Non-Such Lane, Burton, Warwickshire to my son Richard John Baker of Rose Cottage, Hill Street, Minford, Warwickshire or if this should be sold or otherwise disposed of during my lifetime any other land or property owned by me at the date of my death free and discharged from all sums secured thereon by way of mortgage or otherwise absolutely.

I devise and bequeath to my daughter-in-law Mary Anne Baker of Rose Cottage, Hill Street, Minford, Warwickshire my emerald and diamond engagement ring, the oak grandmother clock with brass fixtures standing in the hall of my home, the brooch shaped as an apple with five diamonds, and the sum of £5000.

I devise and bequeath to my grandson Robert Matthew Baker of Rose Cottage, Hill Street, Minford, Warwickshire my stamp collection absolutely.

I devise and bequeath to my grandaughter Amanda Mary Baker of Rose Cottage, Hill Street, Minford, Warwickshire, the remainder of my jewellery not previously disposed of.

I devise and bequeath to my sister Mrs Emily Mary Lewis of 22 Mill Lane, Burton, Warwickshire the sum of £5000, and the picture entitled 'Roses in Bloom' painted by William Lewis and currently hanging in the library of my house.

(I) I devise and bequeath the residue and remainder of my estate both real and personal to my husband James Arthur Baker of Broadwood, Non-Such Lane, Burton, Warwickshire absolutely if he shall survive me by thirty days. If he shall not survive me by thirty days then I devise and bequeath all my real and personal estate whatsoever and wheresoever to be divided equally among those of my grandchildren whosoever shall be living at the date of my death.

(J) In witness hereof I have set my hand this day and year first written.

Edith Mary Baker [signature]

Signed by the said testator in the presence of us present at the same time and by us in her presence

Catherine Mary Brown [signature]
High Street,
Burton,
Warwickshire
(Solicitor)

John Henry Willis [signature]
High Street,
Burton,
Warwickshire
(Solicitor)

Notes

1. If you were going to appoint only, say, a firm of solicitors as executors then the first paragraph would have to read:

'I appoint the partners at the date of my death in the firm of Messrs Blogham and Sons of High Street, Minford, Warwickshire (hereinafter called my trustees) to be executors of this my will. The executors and trustees shall be entitled to charge [insert charge if necessary] and be paid out of the residue of my estate all professional and other charges for all business or acts done by them in connection with this my will.'

Do, however, ask any professionals what charges they are likely to make. If it is to be a percentage of the value of the estate then you can insert this figure in the appropriate space as noted above.

2. If your children were to be the sole beneficiaries of your estate you would need to insert the following clause immediately after the executor's clause (D).

'I devise and bequeath all my real and personal estate whatsoever and wheresoever to my children [name] of [address] and [name] of [address] absolutely if they shall survive me by thirty days.'

You would also need to insert the provision that should your main and sole beneficiaries not survive you by 30 days you would leave your estate to someone else. An example of this would be:

'If they shall not survive me by thirty days I devise and bequeath all my said estate whatsoever and wheresoever to [name] of [address] absolutely or in the event of him not surviving me for the aforesaid period I direct that my said estate is [insert here what you wish to do with your estate in these circumstances].'

3. In the event that you wish to leave a life interest to your wife (or husband) then the following paragraph should be inserted in the will in place of the paragraph after the executor's clause (D). As life interest clauses can cause disharmony because they are restrictive, careful consideration needs to be given before inserting one.

'I devise and bequeath all my real and personal estate whatsoever and wheresoever to my trustees upon trust to sell to postpone sale and to invest the proceeds thereof and apply the income for the benefit of my husband [name] of [address] until he dies or remarries whichever is the sooner. Thereafter in the event of his death or remarriage the proceeds are to be divided amongst such of my children [names] of [addresses] as shall be living at the date of my husband's death or remarriage absolutely.'

As you can see from the sample will, you can made as many and as varied 'dispositions' as you wish, provided that you clearly state that you 'give and bequeath' or 'devise and bequeath' whatever legacy you wish to give them.

Presuming that you wish to make various gifts but that the remainder of your estate is to be divided between your husband and son, in other words neatly cutting the residue of your estate in half, the following clause would need to be inserted (I).

'I devise and bequeath half of my real and personal estate whatsoever and wheresoever to my husband [name] of [address] absolutely if he shall survive me by thirty days and the other half of my real and personal estate whatsoever and wheresoever to my son [name] of [address] in equal shares absolutely. If either shall not survive me by thirty days then his share shall accrue to my estate and be given absolutely to the survivor.

If you are a widow or widower with a child under the age of eighteen then you may wish to take this age factor into account and insert the following clause (instead of (F)).

'I devise and bequeath all my real and personal estate whatsoever and wheresoever to my trustees [names and addresses] upon trust to pay my funeral and testamentary expenses and to stand in possession of the residue of my estate and apply the income therefrom for the benefit of my son [name] of [address] until he reaches the age of twenty-one and thereafter to him absolutely.'

It would be prudent, in case of a tragedy, to insert the following statement underneath the one noted above in case the minor should also not survive but leave children.

'I devise and bequeath all my real and personal estate whatsoever and wheresoever to my son [name] of [address] and in the event of his death before me for his share to pass to such of his children who shall be living at the time of my death.'

As you can see in the main will, when leaving a legacy to a relative, it is best that you specify what that relationship is. So, for example, if the person is a half sister then the will should specify this relationship, ie 'to my sister of the half blood'. Always try to give the full and correct names of beneficiaries rather than 'pet' names and always give the last known (or current) address.

When leaving money to charities, note clearly the full name and correct address of that charity along with the bequests that you desire to make. Often charities, knowing that you wish to contribute, will supply you with a separate legacy form. It is not, however, advisable to use this. Instead, include the legacy with the others in your will.

If you are a partner in a business then this fact should be noted in the will and a partnership agreement should have been drawn up on the commencement of that business. This agreement should stipulate the precise division of the firm's shares or your interest. In a two-man partnership if one partner dies leaving the other half of the business (noted as his property) to his wife then the surviving partner has two options. First, he can agree to buy out the deceased partner's share, or second, he can take his partner's spouse in as a new partner. If the later instance occurs then a new partnership document must be drawn up. In the case of the former the surviving partner would have to have sufficient funds available to buy out the wife's share. Of course, the partnership agreement can include contingency plans to ensure that the surviving partner keeps the business afloat.

Lastly, if you wish to leave your body or parts of your body for medical research or for 'spare part' surgery, then in addition to carrying a donor card, you can insert the following clause, see (E). Of course, do notify your next of kin of this wish.

'I desire and authorise after my death the use of part [state which] or parts of my body for medical research.'

What is a codicil?

When making a simple alteration to your will or when revoking any provision made in it, a codicil can be used. If you wish to change executors or to name a person not previously included as a beneficiary in your will, then again a codicil can be used.

By adding this supplement to your will you can include new instructions and delete old ones without having to go through the task of rewriting the whole of the will.

You can make as many codicils as you wish. However, too many might make your affairs complicated and it might be easier and simpler to rewrite your will. As a rule, if any matter is not straightforward then a new will should be written rather than relying on a codicil.

To be valid a codicil has to be signed by yourself and witnessed (not necessarily by the original witnesses of your will) in exactly the same way as your will. Again, as with your will, these witnesses must not be beneficiaries of your will nor must their spouses be named.

A codicil takes the following form:

'I [name] of [address] declare this to be a first [or second or third etc] codicil to my will dated that fourteenth day of October one thousand nine hundred and eighty-eight.

I revoke the previous bequest to my neighbour Mrs Sally Seward of 22 Highcliffe Road, Weston on Sea of £500 and I in turn give £500 to Mrs Lucy May Smith of 13 Sellwright Road, Weston on Sea.

In all other respects I confirm my will.

This codicil is date the twenty-second day of January one thousand nine hundred and eighty-nine.

Signed by [testator's signature]

Signed by the said testator in our presence and then by us in his presence

(Here the witnesses sign their names giving their full addresses and occupations.)

David Smith, High Street, Weston on Sea (Shopkeeper)

Phillip Lewis, Seacliffe, Burton on Sea (Retired Naval Officer)

If you do make a codicil ensure that you refer to your will stating the correct date of that will.

6

A QUESTION
OF TAX

In his 1986 Budget the Chancellor officially changed the name of capital transfer tax to that of inheritance tax. A further but more fundamental change took place in his 1988 Budget with regard to capital taxes in the United Kingdom. From the 15 March 1988 whoever lived in the United Kingdom would have their estate – upon death – taxed once assets exceeded £110,000. Any monies over that amount would be applicable to a single band of inheritance tax at the rate of 40 per cent.

This change drastically reduced the potential liability that existed before that date on the larger estates. Therefore this has to be a prime motivator in replanning your estate to take full advantage of the current state of tax planning. For example, before the 1988 Budget a widow with assets of £700,000 would have paid £324,000 in inheritance tax on her death. The example below assumes that she had made no gifts over the past seven years.

	£
House	250,000
Stocks and shares	300,000
Personal effects	100,000
Building society deposits	50,000
Total value of estate	£700,000

In tax terminology, gifts are meant as a sum of money or a portion of her estate given to anyone before her death. Provided that seven years had elapsed from the time of making the gift until her death then no tax would be payable on the value of that gift. If death occurred during that period then a portion of tax would be payable on the value of the gift.

Table 1 - Prior to 15.3.1988

Cumulative chargeable transfer	Rate of tax	Tax on band	Cumulative tax
0 – £90,000	NIL	NIL	NIL
£90,000 – £140,000	30%	£15,000	£15,000
£140,001 – £200,000	40%	£32,000	£47,000
£200,001 – £330,000	50%	£55,000	£102,000
£330,001 – £700,000	60%	£222,000	£324,000

Effective rate of tax £324,000/£700,000 × 100 = 46.63 per cent.

On or after Budget day, 15 March 1988, the tax was reduced by 13 per cent to £236,000, which meant a saving of £88,000. This would have been calculated as follows:

Table 2 - After 15.3.1988

Cumulative chargeable transfer	Rate of tax	Tax on band	Cumulative tax
0 – £110,000	NIL	NIL	NIL
£110,000 – £700,000	40%	£236,000	£236,000

Effective rate of tax £236,000/£700,000 × 100 = 33.71 per cent.

Currently any personal gifts made during a person's lifetime in excess of the annual or other specific exemptions, such as gifts on marriage, are known as 'potentially exempt transfers'. These transfers are subject to inheritance tax only if the person who makes the gift dies within a seven-year period from the time of making the gift. Tax is reduced on a sliding scale depending on how many years have elapsed before the donor's death. The following table shows you what that scale is:

Table 3

Years before death	Percentage of death rate (%)
0 – 3	100
3 – 4	80
4 – 5	60
5 – 6	40
6 – 7	20

The earlier a person starts to plan their estate for inheritance tax the better. This planning helps to reduce any adverse effect the tax may make on the estate, either from a change in government or a premature death.

Equalisation of estates

The first basic step for planning of an estate, assuming you are married, is equalisation of the estate between husband and wife. Each spouse should leave at least the amount of the nil rate band (currently £110,000) directly to their children, close relatives (other than husband or wife) or indeed to a close friend. So what must be upmost in your mind is to use the amount allowed for in the nil rate band.

Take the following example. A couple have a combined estate of £250,000. Should the husband die first and leave all his money to his wife who, sadly, dies six months later then, on the value of the estate, tax of £56,000 would have to be paid. No tax would be payable on the first death as transfers between husband and wife are exempt. However, on her death the following calculation applies:

Table 4

Estate   £250,000
Tax   £56,000

Transfer	Slice	Rate	Tax on slice	Total tax
0 – £110,000	£110,000	0%	NIL	NIL
£110,000 – £250,000	£140,000	40%	£56,000	£56,000

Effective rate £56,000/£250,000 = 22.40 per cent.

Because of this charge you might be tempted to say 'there is now no need to plan for inheritance tax'. But if you are in the fortunate position of having that amount of assets, effectively you will be writing your will as, 'to my friends and relatives I leave £464,000 and to the government I leave £246,000'. You may, of course, feel generously inclined to the tax authorities, but 40 per cent still bites deep in to any one's estate!

On the other hand, had the husband and wife planned their estate and the husband had left £110,000 to his son with the balance of £15,000 to his wife, then no tax would be paid on his death and only £12,000 tax would be payable on the death of his wife six months later.

Table 5

Wife's estate £140,000 (£125,000 = self, £15,000 ex-husband's estate)

Tax = £12,000

Transfer	Slice	Rate	Tax on slice	Total tax
0 – £110,000	£110,000	0%	NIL	NIL
£110,000 – £140,000	£30,000	40%	£12,000	£12,000

Effective rate £12,000/£250,000 × 100 = 4.8 per cent.

By this simple planning route £44,000 of tax has been saved. This equalisation of assets between spouses not only saves on inheritance tax but, if a future government were ever to introduce an annual wealth tax, equalisation would minimise the effect of this tax as well.

No matter what you decide on, eventually the government will change and the question of capital taxes – limits and/or methods of calculation – will probably be cause for thought once more. The need therefore exists to plan your estate effectively if you think that it will exceed the current tax band of £110,000. Remember, of course, that this band depends on the Chancellor's discretion and the amount will no doubt be adjusted in subsequent Budgets.

'But my estate isn't going to exceed £110,000.' When was the last time you valued all your possessions? What is the current value of your house? Have you recently taken out an addition to your life insurance policy? Have you increased your pension contributions? Has an endowment policy recently been paid? What savings and investments do you now hold? Leaving aside the possibility of your being a beneficiary of someone else's estate, does your revised calculation now show your estate to be worth over £110,000? Many people revising the value of their assets are pleasantly surprised.

Settlements

Instead of using outright gifts to reduce the value of your estate you may instead prefer to use *settlements*. It was the 1986 Finance

Act that introduced inheritance tax, which replaced the old capital transfer tax. Under this new Act, gifts made into *accumulation and maintenance settlements* or gifts into *interest in possession trusts* are, as with outright gifts, seen 'potentially exempt transfers' which means there is no inheritance tax liability, provided the person making a gift survives a period of seven years after making the settlement.

If you have children, or indeed if you have grandchildren, then accumulation and maintenance settlements are especially suitable. Under this type of settlement the beneficiary will receive income from the trust as a right and by the age of 25 receives the entire holding. There are certain rules to follow when considering making this settlement and these are:

1. The beneficiary is entitled to the property of the trust or to an interest in possession on attaining a specified age, which must not exceed 25.
2. The income from the trust must either be accumulated within the fund or applied for the benefit of the beneficiary and
3. Either
   (a) not more than 25 years have elapsed since the settlement was first made, or
   (b) all the beneficiaries are grandchildren of a common grandparent.

Provided that these conditions can be satisfied then all gifts made into the trust are seen as 'potentially exempt transfers' and escape the periodic charge applicable to large *discretionary trusts*. An additional benefit is that there is no inheritance tax charge when the beneficiaries finally inherit all the assets.

There is, as with most things, a minus side. This downside is that if any of the beneficiaries are your own children under the age of 18 and receive income from the settlement, then this income is added to your own and you in turn are liable to tax, potentially at the top rate of 40 per cent.

The use of *small discretionary settlements* can be most beneficial. These settlements provide a greater degree of flexibility on the distribution of income and capital, provided that the initial amount settled into them is less than the nil inheritance tax rate band, which is currently £110,000. There is no inheritance tax to pay upon setting up the trust. A *discretionary trust* is one of the few areas of tax planning that does give rise to a life time charge[1] if the

---

[1] A lifetime charge – as opposed to a death charge – is one which is raised for payment during your lifetime.

amount settled exceeds a person's chargeable nil rate band, but the tax payable is at half the death rate, in other words 20 per cent.

Of all the taxes applied throughout the United Kingdom, inheritance tax is the one which, provided careful planning has been done early enough, can be legally avoided.

Each year everyone is allowed an annual tax exemption of £3000 against captial gifts. If you do not take advantage of this annual exemption it remains available to be carried forward, but only for a further 12 months. It is therefore important to use this annual exemption each year. Other tax exemptions are noted on the following pages.

Transfers between husband and wife

The transfer of assets upon death between husband and wife, provided that the recipient is domiciled in the United Kingdom, is exempt from inheritance tax. If a person is not domiciled here then only £50,000 is exempt.

Domicile

The understanding of the tax definition of the word 'domicile' is important, although it is a concept of general law and not tax law.

Your domicile is the place which you regard as your permanent home and which you consider to be the country with which you are most clearly connected and, if abroad, can be the place you intend to return to. You can only be domiciled in one place at a time and must positively establish your domicility by setting foot in the country concerned. To make matters more complicated there are three different domiciles: domicile of origin, domicile of choice and domicile of dependency.

Domicile of origin usually follows that of your father at the time of your birth, unless your father had died. If this had happened then you would take on the domicile of your mother. Illegitimate children usually take the domicile'of their mother.

Domicile of choice is the choosing of a new country to live in and to make your new life in – having permanently and *absolutely* abandoned the old country – and having no intention of returning to your old home.

You can have numerous domiciles of choice throughout your life provided that in each case you abandon the old place of domicile with the intention of permanently making your home in the new country of domicile and actually going to live there.

Domicile of dependency means that if you have a child under the age of 16 (or a mentally handicapped child) then that child takes on the domicile of the person on whom they are dependent. Deemed domicile – if you live in the United Kingdom after 9 December 1974 for taxation purposes you retain domicile in the United Kingdom for three years after establishing domicile elsewhere. The tax authorities also deem you 'domicile' if you have lived in the United Kingdom for most of the past 20 years of tax assessments.

Gifts

SMALL GIFTS
The outright gift to any one person up to the value of £250 is exempt from tax.

EXPENDITURE OUT OF INCOME
This can sometimes be difficult to establish as not only does the transfer have to come out of your normal expenditure but there must also be an element of regularity. In other words, if ever you give it bi-monthly then this procedure must be kept up. The premiums for a life policy that have been written under trust, for example, will be treated as a gift for the purpose of inheritance tax, unless it can be shown that it falls within the normal expenditure rules as a gift out of income. To qualify under this exemption it has to come out of your 'after tax' income and still leave you with enough money to maintain yourself in your usual mode of living.

GIFTS IN CONSIDERATION OF MARRIAGE
This is limited to £5000 if the donor is a parent of one of the marriage partners. It reduces to £2500 if the donor is a grandparent of either of the marriage partners and again reduces to £1000 if the gift is from anyone else.

GIFTS TO CHARITIES
There is no limit to the amount of money that can be donated to a registered charity free of tax.

GIFTS TO POLITICAL PARTIES
Again, there is no limit to the amount that can be donated to a

political party provided that the party has at least two current sitting Members of Parliament or has polled not less than 150,000 voters for its candidates at the last general election.

GIFTS FOR THE PUBLIC'S BENEFIT OR FOR NATIONAL PURPOSES
There is no limit to the amount of money that can be donated, tax free, for these purposes.

By taking advantage of these exemptions, even if there were to be a change in government, gifts that were made at the time of exemptions should prove to be safe from any later changes that might be legislated.

When is inheritance tax applied?

Inheritance tax, if you are domiciled in the United Kingdom, or deemed to be domiciled, applies at death to all your property wherever it is situated globally once your assets exceed £110,000, current level. If you are not domiciled here then inheritance tax will only apply to your assets which are situated in the United Kingdom. Assets mean property as well as personal effects with a quantifiable value. It is important to know whether you are deemed to be domiciled in the United Kingdom for inheritance tax purposes. The taxation officials have certain rules which apply to the definition of the term domicile. They are:

1. You are domiciled here on or after 10 December 1974 and within three years preceding death.
2. Resident here on or before 10 December 1974 and in not less 17 years of the previous 20 years.

The Isle of Man and the Channel Islands, for the purpose of inheritance tax, are not part of the United Kingdom, but all other parts, Scotland, Northern Ireland, Wales and England are taxed under the same rules.

To change one's domicile is not an easy matter as you are actually born with a domicility and as previously stated, normally that is considered to be the same domicile as your father. In order to change your domicile to one of domicile of choice you have to have resided in your new chosen country for a considerable period of time, having proved an intent to live there by purchasing a new home. It also helps to marry a native of that country and to develop business interests there. Arrangements should be made so that your body is buried in that country and indeed, that all connections with your former country of domicile be severed, even down to club membership.

Funeral expenses and any debts owed by you at the time of your death are deducted from the value of your estate before calculating the amount of tax payable. Tax must be paid before probate is granted.

What can be achieved if no prior planning has been done?

DEED OF VARIATION

If someone has died within a two-year period then their will can effectively be re-written to take advantage of the £110,000 nil rate inheritance tax band. This is done by means of a document called 'a deed of family arrangement'. This document is a very valuable tool in inheritance tax planning but it has to be remembered that:

(a) it can only be made within two years of a person's death;
(b) the Inland Revenue must be notified within six months from the date of variation;
(c) the deed of variation cannot be made if any of the legacies under the terms of the will have actually been disposed of; and
(d) all beneficiaries must agree to this being done.

Indeed, the prime reason for using a deed of variation or deed of family arrangement is because the estate in its present form is not tax efficient and a deed is made to make it more tax efficient.

Before having a deed of variation drawn up all the beneficiaries under the will must get together for common purpose and agree to the terms of the will. For example, suppose you die leaving the bulk of your estate to your wife but with the stipulation that upon her death a small portion is to go to one of her cousins. Because she is the sole beneficiary of your will your wife can amend it. You will certainly need the services of a solicitor in drawing up a deed.

The deed of variation takes its name because you are altering the variation to the terms of the will. Once a deed of variation has been accepted it is, in effect, taken as the ultimate varied will for tax purposes and treated as if it were the original one.

The Inland Revenue have four rules that must be observed before a deed of variation is accepted.

1. A notice in writing must be made by the beneficiaries under the terms of the will at the date of death.

2. This written notification must be made within two years after the person's death.
3. The deed of variation must clearly set out the altered parts of the will and the new destination of the property.
4. Written notice must be given to the Inland Revenue, otherwise it will not count as a transfer upon death for tax purposes.

Another example of the usefulness of a deed of variation is if your estate had gone to your surviving spouse (*Note,* no tax is payable upon transfer between husband and wife) then the first £110,000 could be diverted to other member of your family, upon all concerned agreeing to this, and still not incur any inheritance tax. In large estates, a deed of family arrangement could also include gifts to charities which, as noted previously, are free from inheritance tax.

But suppose you die without making a will? Even if a person has died intestate, provided the main beneficiary, ie the surviving spouse or children, agrees, then a deed of variation can be entered into.

Before deciding to take this step and going to a solicitor, the main beneficiaries should first consult a tax expert and ascertain how much tax could be saved. If the amount is small then the fees for rearranging affairs might be as much as the tax payable.

Business property relief

Other tax reliefs that can be used include business property relief. This not only includes a business or part of it but also shares in certain companies. However, it excludes those in property or investment companies. This relief comes in the form of a discount in the value of the assets as follows:

1. By 50 per cent of the whole or part of a business or company shares valued on a controlling basis, and by 25 per cent in holdings in an unquoted traded company.
2. By 30 per cent in buildings, plant and machinery used by a company controlled by you or a business in which you are a partner.
3. By 30 per cent for a minority holding of shares in an upquoted trading company. After 17 March 1987 a holding of 25 per cent carries a 50 per cent tax relief.

Provided the recipient still owns the property – which must still be in use as a business and as such can genuinely be termed 'business property' – then even if the gift falls into tax charge following your death within the seven years, it will still qualify for business property relief.

Agricultural property relief

There is another relief available called an agricultural property relief. This applies if you have either occupied a property for the purpose of farming and had farmed it for at least two years or had owned it for at least seven years. If the property has vacant possession then the relief is 50 per cent of the value. For the purpose of the definition of 'relief', the term farming also includes stud farming. The relief is reduced to 30 per cent if you do not own the freehold to the property.

Related property rules

The value of any shares held in a company can be increased because of what is known as the 'related property' rules. Under these rules your holding is combined with another and the appropriate portion of the value of the combined holding is taken against the value for inheritance tax purposes. For example, if you owned 35 per cent of the shares in your family's unquoted trading company and your wife held another 35 per cent, bringing the total value held by you both to 70 per cent, this would give you full control of the business and much more than a minority holding of a single 35 per cent. What it would mean is that your shares would be valued at 50 per cent of the joint holding of 70 per cent.

Ignoring business property relief, because inheritance tax is payable on death based on the full asset value, in order to plan effectively you should not wait until the family firm has become successful before transferring shares to younger members of the family. Instead, you should transfer the shares to your children before the value increases. The best time to do this is when the company is first formed.

Although chargeable transfers have to be reported to the Inland Revenue within 12 months of a person's death, interest on late payment of inheritance tax starts to be charged from the end of the month in which the death occurred. For example, if Great Uncle Harry died in October 1988 and inheritance tax was not settled by the end of April 1989, then interest on late payment would be charged.

The tax payable on any land or business assets which Great Uncle Harry may have owned, including controlling shares, may be paid over 10 years, interest free. It sometimes happens that shares are sold within 12 months of a person's death for less than the stated probate value. The person liable to inheritance tax can claim that the sale price be substituted for the original probate value provided that the proceeds are not later reinvested into that same company.

Suppose that you were selling Great Uncle Harry's shares, the probate value being £7000, and because of the fall in the stock market you have only managed to obtain £5000 then if you are liable to the inheritance tax on his estate you can claim back the sale price less the original probate value, provided that the proceeds are not then reinvested into the same company.

A similar rule applies to land. If land is sold for less than the probate value within a three-year period, then the sale price can be substituted for the probate price. If Great Uncle Harry had received money from someone else's estate on which he had paid inheritance tax, provided it had occurred over the last five years the following deduction of the original tax is given:

Table 6

	%
0 – 1 years	100
1 – 2 years	80
2 – 3 years	60
3 – 4 years	40
4 – 5 years	20

Disposing of an asset

If you, as a donor, dispose of an asset to another person but retain an interest in that asset, then for inheritance tax purposes it is not seen as being an effective transfer as it has a 'prior reservation'. Under the old capital taxes rules a popular method of tax planning used to be for a couple to give shares in their main residence to their children as tenants in common which they then continue to occupy. This transfer substantially reduced the value of the estate. With the introduction of reservation rules it was first thought that this method would be ineffective as the donors would continue to occupy the whole of the house including the gifted share. However, during the Finance Bill 1986 a government spokesman went on record to state that the reservation rules would not apply in the following circumstances:

Elderly parents make unconditional gifts of individual shares of their house to their children and the parents and the children continue to occupy the property as the family home, such owner bearing his or her running costs. In those circumstances it is thought that the donors' occupation is termed as one for full consideration whereby, because each has a use of each others part of the house and each bears the cost of maintenance then the reservation rules can be set aside.

In many circumstances, however, it would not be practical for the beneficiaries also to reside in the property so that this line of tax planning has, within certain limitations, now been blocked.

As trusts can be useful tax planning vehicles with regard to inheritance tax, it is worthwhile considering the different types of trusts and how effective they can be in inheritance tax planning. However, if you are going to set up a trust then you must go to a solicitor and ask for his assistance.

Interest in possession trusts

Although not defined in the tax legislation, an 'interest in possession' exists when someone is absolutely entitled to the trust's income. When that interest comes to an end because of the life tenant's death, the assets of the trust are added together with the person's free estate (in other words, whatever is owned outside the life tenancy) to determine the total amount of inheritance tax payable. The trustees will become liable to tax on a pro-rata share of the total tax payable. If you dispose of your interest during your life time, then the value of the trust is treated by the tax authorities as a life time gift and would be taxed according to the life-time tax rates applicable to yourself. This means that if your tax rate is 40 per cent then whatever assets are yours and incur inheritance tax these will also be taxed at 40 per cent.

There are three occasions when no inheritance tax will be payable, and these are:

1. Where you have the interest in possession and become absolutely entitled to the assets of the trust.
2. Where the property of that trust reverts to the settler's spouse (in other words, the person who has made the trust out) during the settlement life time or if death occurs within a two-year period.
3. Where the life tenant is the surviving widow or widower of

the settlement and the old estate duty (pre-1974) was paid when he or she died.

Children: accumulation and maintenance settlements

This type of settlement is an extension of a discretionary settlement with inheritance tax advantages provided the following criteria can be satisfied:

1. At least one of the beneficiaries will become entitled to at least the income from the trust if not the capital at the age of 25.
2. The income in the meantime must be accumulated or applied towards the education of the child or children.
3. No more than 25 years can elapse since the settlement was first made and all the beneficiaries are the grandchildren of common grandparents. In such a case there is no tax payable when setting up the trust (assuming that the donor survives for a period of 7 years) although there is a 10-year anniversary charge.

Most people are pleasantly surprised when working out the valuation of their estate. How to value an estate can be seen in Chapter 10. It is important to have an overall value of your estate in order to minimise the tax liabilities which your estate or beneficiaries will face.

By planning in advance, for example by equalising the estate and the income produced by it, you can ensure that your estate – and your family's affairs – are in a more tax-efficient position. Equalising assets also has an added benefit in that in 1990 a new tax treatment is due to be introduced for wives.

Discretionary trusts

With a discretionary settlement no one has an interest in possession as seen by the tax authority and inheritance tax is payable in the following circumstances:

1. When capital is first put into the settlement.
2. Where capital is distributed to the beneficiary or beneficiaries.
3. On the tenth anniversary of the settlement, tax is payable on 15 per cent of the death rate.

It is not within the capacity of this book to deal comprehensively with trusts as an entity as they are a personal financial vehicle to each individual's estate and should be individually planned. If you wish to draw up a trust then you whould go to a solicitor as well as a tax consultant for assistance. However, as a tax vehicle, a two-year discretionary trust will be briefly discussed.

This is a very flexible type of trust and can be used, for example, if you wish your estate to be held in trust for your wife and/or children for a period of two years from your death. During that time capital from the trust can be paid out to trust members at the executor's discretion. It means that your wife and children can get money when they most need it without incurring a heavy tax burden. The decision as to who needs what and when allows the trust's executor to distribute the estate as tax-effeciently as possible.

Jointly owned property

Property can be assigned in two ways. The first is in a joint tenancy and the second is in a tenancy-in-common. In a joint tenancy, when the co-owner dies the surviving co-owner automatically takes over the deceased's half irrespective of provisions in his will. Of course, a solicitor should have been used to adjust the property's title deeds to this effect.

Tenancy-in-common means that the deceased's share of the house passes to the estate under the terms of the will. From a tax point of view, whether the husband inherits his share from his wife or *vice versa*, if the property is jointly owned by them then the share will be exempt from inheritance tax under the 'surviving spouse' exemption. If the property is owned jointly by two friends or, say, by a mother and son, then the share will become liable to inheritance tax as it is not applicable under the above stated exemption.

If a mother wanted her son eventually to inherit her half of the house (held as tenants-in-common) then she could write in her will that a life interest goes to her husband but that on his death her son receives her share. By doing this she ensures that her son eventually inherits her half. If, for example, she were a co-owner in a joint tenancy, then after her death it would pass automatically to the husband, and if he remarried his new wife would become entitled to the whole of the house upon the father's death unless he made a will to the contrary. This could not happen under a tenancy-in-common as the husband and the new wife would live in the house but on the husband's death his first wife's share in the property would pass to her son.

How is tax paid?

When the executor or administrator has completed the Inland Revenue forms received from and returned to the Probate Registry (or in Scotland from the Commissary Office), the Registry will, if it is appropriate, send the forms to the Capital Taxes Office at Minford House, Rockley Road, London W14 0DF (Tel: 01-603 4622). Here the information contained in the forms will be assessed to see whether or not any tax is immediately payable. Tax due on an estate other than house, property or land or share in a private company, must be paid before the grant of probate or letters of administration is issued.

Usually, the executor is informed by the Probate Registry – on behalf of the Inland Revenue – if any tax is due and the amount. If the assessment is incorrect or you can not agree with this assessment you should write immediately to the tax authorities stating the reason why you do not agree with their assessment. If the grant has not as yet been issued by the Probate Registry then you should write to them in the first instance. Always quote the reference number given on any replies received from the authorities. If dealing with the Inland Revenue direct then you should note all the details of the will, for example, the deceased's name, address, the date probate was granted and what Probate Registry was dealing with matters.

As can be imagined, a difficulty arises when the testator has not taken into account the value of the estate grossed up. For example, say you left £130,000 outright and had distributed this same amount under the terms of your will making no allowance for tax to be deducted from your estate. Your beneficiaries would only receive a portion of your written declaration because tax would first have to be paid before probate and distribution took place. So a word of warning, inheritance tax can damage your wealth!

To make these calculations simpler, the Revenue have produced tax tables showing what inheritance tax is due on different amounts of grossed up estates. Once you have valued your estate it may be worthwhile to ask your local HM Inspector of Taxes' office to forward a copy to you so that you can make sure that your calculations are correct. (See page 95 for the table on how to calculate inheritance tax.)

Always remember that the Revenue work on the principle that the tax payable on the legacy is an integral part of your estate and in most cases must be paid before distribution can take place.

Insurance against inheritance tax

You can insure your estate against paying inheritance tax but be warned, it is expensive. Basically, the insurance companies work on the principle that the older you are the higher the premiums become as the day of your 'parting is that much closer.

It could be argued that, for the increased premiums asked, if the same amount were put aside and invested then this extra money could achieve much the same end in alleviating the tax burden when it falls. Of course, the best 'insurance policy' is to make sure that you have taken all necessary estate planning measures.

7

DEALING WITH PERSONAL TAX MATTERS AFTER DEATH

The administrator, shortly after the death of an individual who has died without making a will, has to settle the deceased's personal tax liabilities. He has to see that any income tax, capital gains tax or inheritance tax liabilities are paid to the Inland Revenue. Handling these affairs can not only mean paying out money to clear the tax bill but also applying for a refund of tax from the Inspector of Taxes. Whichever applies, the amounts are seen as either a liability or an asset of the deceased person's estate as at the date of death and will affect the amount of inheritance tax due.

As executor, you should be aware that there are a number of time limitations set by the tax authority for raising an assessment for tax on the deceased's estate.

1. Under Section 40(1) Taxes Management Act 1970, the Inland Revenue must raise the assessment within three years of the end of the tax year in which the death took place. In other words, if a person died on 1 March 1988 then the assessment must be raised by the Revenue no later than 5 April 1991.
2. Under Section 34(1) Taxes Management Act 1970, any assessment raised within the three-year period mentioned in 1. can only relate to the deceased person's six previous taxable

years. In other words, if a person died on 6 January 1989 (this would fall within the 1988/89 tax year) the Revenue could raise a tax assessment(s) for any (or all) of the previous six years prior to his death.

3. If the Inland Revenue can show that tax has been lost to the Crown by 'wilful default or fraud' then the Inland Revenue may raise an assessment on the executor within the previous stated three years relating to any tax year. (A tax year is seen as 12 full months running from 6 April in the first year to 5 April in the following year.) The Revenue's assessment starts with the three years and ends within the six years from the date of death.

In the income tax year in which the death took place, the deceased person will be assessed for tax under various schedules right up to the date of death. There is no apportionment of income in income tax law. For example, income from property assessed under income tax, schedule A is assessed on rents due to the deceased prior to the date of death regardless of whether the money has been received before or after the date of death. The normal cessation rules apply. In other words, income is assessable to income tax schedule D, cases I to V, and any amounts that are received under the deduction of basic rate tax, ie dividend income from shares, will only form part of the deceased person's income if the payment date shown on the dividend voucher falls before the date of death.

However, it does not matter if the payment date on the dividend voucher falls after the date of death. In this instance, the payment becomes income received during the period of administration and therefore there is no question of time apportionment. This makes life somewhat simpler as there is, in general executorship law, the assessment of income tax in the year of death, and this is a relatively simple matter.

How does this affect the surviving partner's tax position?

HUSBAND

The total income of both husband and wife is assessed on the husband up to the date of his death. This assessment qualifies him for a full year's married man's allowance, which is currently (1988/89) £4095. His wife qualifies for maximum wife's earned income allowance of £2605 on her earnings up to the date of her husband's death.

From the date of death, the widow become a taxpayer in her own right and from that date receives a full year's single person's allowance, currently £2605. This allowance remains for the entire tax year. For example, if the husband had died in September, then the wife would be entitled to the entire £2605 from September through to the following 5 April. It would not be based on the tax year, ie 6 April to 5 April in the following year. The extent of this benefit therefore depends on the time of death.

In addition to this allowance, the widow is entitled to a widow's bereavement allowance which amounts to £1490. This amount is allowed in the year her husband died and in the following year, provided she has not remarried. If there are any children under the age of 16 at the beginning of the tax year or if they are in full-time education, then the widow also qualifies for additional personal allowance, currently £1490.

A widow's income may include that from her late husband's estate. This is dealt with in more detail later in this chapter. So the total allowances that a widow can receive if she has not remarried and has children under the age of 16 is £5585.

WIFE

As long as the wife is alive at the start of the tax year, irrespective of the date of her death during that year, the husband will qualify for a full year's married man's allowance of £4095. As with the wife's circumstances shown previously, if there are any children of their marriage, so long as they are still undergoing full-time education now and in subsequent years, the husband will receive an additional personal allowance currently £1490. This together with his normal single person's allowance of £2605, brings his total allowance to that of a married man, in other words £4095.

The late wife's income up to the date of her death is treated in the usual way by adding its value to that of her husband's income. Any investment income arising from assets held, such as stocks and shares, will be taxed in the hands of her executor and ultimately form part of her husband's income to the extent that he is the ultimate beneficiary.

What is a tax code?

The tax allowances that are given to you are shown in the income tax coding sent to you by the Inland Revenue. If you have any doubts as to its correctness then telephone the Revenue, reiterating your circumstances and the income earned and ask for your code to be checked.

The income tax code shows a figure and a letter. The figure indicates the amount you are allowed to earn before tax and the letter states what category you are in. In this instance, the widow would have an allowance figure of £5585 and would be given a code of 558. This would be followed by the letter L for a single person's or wife's earned income allowance.

Other letters you will come across are:

F which indicates a person who has income which places him between the two tax bands;
H for a married man's allowance or married woman's allowance if the husband does not work;
P for a single person's allowance over the age of 65; V for a married man when one partner is 65 or over;
D if salary exceeds the current basic rate of tax of £19,300;
NT no tax deducted;
OT no personal allowances.

There are two other categories: BR if there is a second job and T which is a confidential category if a person does not want their employer to know what tax code they are on or indicates an age allowance.

Any change in your circumstances should be notified to the Revenue so that your code can be adjusted.

Income tax due during the period of administration

Wherever you live in the United Kingdom, any tax matters mentioned in this book will apply as the Inland Revenue – unlike the Probate Registry or Commissary Offices – cover the whole of Great Britain, except for the Channel Islands and the Isle of Man.

An executor's duties start after a person's death. Often the responsibility for making the funeral arrangements falls on you. Your duties continue throughout the period of administration, collecting the assets, paying the creditors, seeing that specific legacies are paid off and the residuary legatee (the person whom the remainder of the estate goes to) is informed of the balance.

In your final correspondence a letter should be sent to the residuary beneficiary in which you list all the remaining assets available. By doing this the residue is then stated to have been 'ascertained'.

When you consent to the beneficiary taking these assets over it is termed as 'assenting to the residuary bequest'. At the same time as you send this letter you should also send a copy of the estate's accounts and ask the beneficiary to sign them as proof of the formal discharge. When this is done you have effectively ended the period of administration.

It may be that under the terms of the will the deceased created a trust. At this point you, as the executor, cease to be the executor and become the trustee.

From the date of death the executor receives all income which arises from any of the deceased person's estate, some of which will be taxed at source. In other words, the sending organisation will already have deducted tax. This usually happens with building society or bank accounts or dividends gained from company shares. Other income, such as rental from property and so on, is untaxed and is sent directly to the executor. The Inland Revenue will raise an assessment on you in your role as executor of the estate. This does not mean that your own personal tax affairs are affected. Incidentally, irrespective of the number of executors, there is only one assessment raised by the Inland Revenue as the executors are seen by the Revenue as one singular entity.

Although as the executor you are not entitled to claim for a personal allowance on the deceased's behalf, you are entitled to claim for losses made after the person's death while you are running his business. As far as the income tax rules are concerned, the death of a trader and the subsequent passing of his business to a successor normally marks the end or cessation of a trade. However, where a business passes on death to a trader's spouse, then these discontinuation provisions do not apply and she would be assessed for tax on the previous year's basis. In other words, profits in the year ended 30 April 1988 would be assessed to income tax in the tax year 1989/90.

As an executor you can also obtain income tax relief for the estate on interest payments, if those interest payments would have been deducted for tax purposes for the deceased. As an executor you may also have to obtain a loan, using the estate as security, so that the inheritance tax bill can be met. It should be noted that the personal representatives of the deceased can obtain income tax relief on interest paid on a loan within a one-year period of raising that loan, provided it was used to pay for inheritance tax. If the interest cannot be relieved wholly in the year when it is paid then it can either be carried back or forward as required. As an executor, you are never assessed to the higher rates of income tax during the period of administration.

If you continue to run the deceased's business then the profits made become liable to income tax under schedule D, case I or II. If you merely sell off trading stock then there would be no income tax liability whatsoever.

Expenses incurred while administering the estate are not allowable for income tax and must be met from taxed income. Interest on non-payment of inheritance tax (which runs from six months after the end of the month in which the death occurred) is also not considered to be an expense and is therefore not allowable to be set against income tax. Executor's expenses are not considered to be tax deductible, including solicitors' charges.

As seen earlier, dividend income received after the date of death forms part of the income of the estate as it was received during the period of administration. This is so even if the accounting year in which it was declared may have fallen before the date of death. All income received during the period of adminstration is liable to basic rate income tax, which is currently 25 per cent.

If a beneficiary is not liable to income tax because the income is covered by the existing personal allowance, then the income tax deducted by you as the executor can be reclaimed. However, if the beneficiary is in the higher rate of income tax, currently a 40 per cent, then he will have to pay an additional 15 per cent income tax. In other words, 40 per cent minus 25 per cent already deducted.

The distribution of income to a beneficiary

As an executor you should be aware of the implications of distribution of income to the beneficiary. The amount of income to which a legatee becomes entitled depends on the terms of his legacy.

GENERAL LEGACIES

A specific sum of money, say, £5000 or an asset, say, 'my motor car', is referred to as capital matter. As capital matter it means that the person inheriting it is not entitled to any income during the period of administration unless the will directs that interest is to be paid on the legacy. If this is so then the beneficiary is liable to income tax under schedule D, case III on the amount received. This can prove to be expensive from the tax point of view as the estate income has already been taxed once at the basic rate of tax. Once the money has been paid out to the beneficiary, the interest paid out by you on the net amount becomes liable to tax as though it were a gross receipt. This harsh tax treatment also applies to the interest payable to the surviving spouse in intestacy case, (for fuller details of tax applicable in intestacy cases see section 46 of the Administration of Estates Act 1925).

SPECIFIC LEGACIES

This term refers to a gift of, say, £10,000 or say, a gift of 10 per cent of Treasury Stock 1992, and entitles the beneficiary to the interest incurred on a day-to-day basis from the date of death. The Inland Revenue assess this interest under income tax, schedule F. Any interest received prior to the person's death forms part of the residue of the estate.

ANNUITIES

A gift, say, £1000 stipulated in the will to be paid over a specified period of time, say, 20 years from the date of death. On each anniversary of that person's death you, as the executor, would have to distribute £1000 less tax of 25 per cent. The beneficiary would receive £750. As it is paid out of income which has already been taxed at the basic rate of tax the real cost to the estate is only £750. This is in sharp contrast to the general legacy which would have been taxed twice.

THE RESIDUE OF THE ESTATE

The main beneficiary under the terms of the will is entitled to the remainder of the estate and is also entitled to any income received unless it is left in trust. If this is the case then the life tenancy of the residue of the estate is only entitled to the income arising after the person's death.

The tax position in the case of the residue of the estate being given absolutely to the beneficiary is as follows. The residuary income of the estate is the total income less the interest and expenses relating to that income. The total income less tax, at the basic rate, and interest and expenses is then grossed up and forms part of the beneficiary's total income. Each year, you would have to supply him with a certificate of tax deduction (form R185) which the beneficiary can then use to claim back the deducted tax. Where a person has only a life interest in the estate then the tax position is different. The net income for the whole of the administration period, less the interest and expenses etc, is seen to have accrued evenly over the period and the amount is allocated to each tax year and is grossed up to the basic rate of tax for the year applicable. These rates are:

1988/89 25 per cent
1987/88 27 per cent
1986/87 29 per cent
1985/86 30 per cent

Under this rule the amounts may have been taxed on the executor at one rate of basic tax but grossed up on the beneficiary at another rate. Therefore it would be best, if possible, to distribute the estate within a 12-month period after the date of death and avoid letting proceedings be drawn out for subsequent years.

8

WHO CAN YOU GO TO FOR HELP?

Some executors would not consider administering an estate without the help of a solicitor. There might be a number of reasons why, such as complexities arising from property within an estate or the existence of a trust. More to the point, however, an executor might not be able to dedicate the number of man-hours necessary to the task of administering an estate. And, of course, personal grief might play an important role when perhaps the executor feels emotionally unable to cope. If you wish to be excused from acting as executor you must send a formal letter (known as a *letter of renunciation*) to the Probate Registry explaining the reason why you feel you are unable to continue and requesting that you be discharged from these duties. This letter has to be witnessed.

If you are dealing through a solicitor this *letter of renunciation* will be prepared for you, or where a personal application has been made the appropriate format will come from the probate Registry. In the latter case, although the letter has been prepared for you, it will have to be signed by you personally as the person making the application. Should the will be in your posession and you wish to renounce your involvement but do not know of any relatives or beneficiaries of the will and therefore cannot hand it over to them for their own application, then in such a case you can hand it over to your nearest Probate Registry along with your letter of renunciation.

When will you need assistance?

Listed below are a number of foreseeable complications which might necessitate an inexperienced executor applying for professional advice, whether it is for the entire duty or only part of it.

1. If the deceased owned a business or was a partner in a business.
2. Family trusts or life interest.
3. If there are any persons benefiting from the estate who are under the age of 18.
4. Loss of will.
5. The possibility of a distant relative claiming inheritance and possible court action thereafter.
6. An inadequately worded will.
7. Insolvency of the estate.
8. If a property which forms part of the estate has an unregistered title.
9. The possibility that unknown debts may arise.

Most of these points are concerned with the distribution of the estate. Before you actually require help you can start proceedings yourself and speed up the actual obtaining of the grant of probate or letters of administration. This application is a simple matter and then later, if the affairs begin to look complicated, or lack of time or whatever reasons prevents you from continuing, you can seek further advice from a financial adviser, tax consultant or solicitor, whichever profession is appropriate to your needs.

Occasionally, situations arise where it is not considered appropriate for you to obtain a grant through the Personal Applications Department of the Probate Registry. However, it is extremely rare for an application to be refused as 999 out of 1000 are accepted.

Where do you start?

If in doubt about any matters regarding prbate contact the Personal Applications Department of the Probate Registry and talk to the staff at the nearest Registry to you. They are in the best position to advise whether the application may be accepted or whether it would be best to instruct a solicitor. It should be remembered that even solicitors' applications are eventually sent to the Probate Registry for completion, so the staff there are competent to give you advice on most aspects of the procedures.

However, they are not allowed to give actual legal advice outside their field.

Solicitors

When making out a will, if you are self-employed or a partner in a business, or if there is substantial property involved, then you will need to use the services of a solicitor. For example, in a partnership between yourself and another person(s) a document called a *partnership agreement* would need to be drawn up. This would stipulate all business arrangements agreed between you and your partner(s) and state what is to happen when any one of the partners leaves the business or dies. This agreement needs to be drawn up before you go into business and reference to needs to be made in your will.

A solicitor's help would also be necessary if you wanted a trust to be drawn up or if you were in an insurance syndicate. In such cases the estate is likely to be complicated and you will definitely need help to pull all the matters together to make them more manageable to administer after your death.

In the case of intestacy, as an executor you might need a solicitor, especially if complications arise, such as difficulties in tracing missing relatives or living relatives residing overseas. This problem is a fairly common one and solicitors know the best ways to have relatives traced.

Solicitors will, if you wish, also keep your will on their premises if they have drawn it up for you or if you are a regular client.

The benefit of using solicitors as opposed to other professional advisers is that their 'watchdog', the Law Society, keeps a close eye on solicitors' actions. For example, if you consider that you have been overcharged you can write asking for its opinion.

Solicitors charge for drawing up a will and this cost can range upwards from £40, depending upon complexities within the estate and the time which has to be spent. If they handle probate then a fee will also be charged. This fee is now based on the time spent and not on a portion of the estate's value. Make sure that you do ask how much this is likely to be. Naturally, you have to be realistic when judging how much the bills should be; like everyone else, solicitors have to earn a crust too!

The more complicated and lengthy a will is, the higher the charge will be. A word of advice; if your will is likely to be complicated or there are any unusual circumstances, then go to a solicitor for help. In these instances it would be unfortunate to follow the DIY approach and fail to achieve your aims either through a technicality or through inaccurate or poor wording.

Incidentally, the Law Society now sells a document called a 'Personal Assets Log', which can be used to list the location of all your important papers whether it is your will or the deed to your property. Whether or not you decide to use the log, it is a good idea to make known to your immediate family the location of all relevant documents.

Another instance where you could benefit from professional advice is in the case of intestacy if the estate is valued at over £75,000 where there are children or issue. By current law, the surviving spouse inherits a life interest in half of the property over that figure of £75,000 and the children receive the other half.

Ambiguity in the meaning or irregularity in the terms of the will gives rise to other instances where professional advice is needed. But again, this need not stop you from initially taking the grant as a personal applicant.

If a person died with debts exceeding assets, despite a will having been made, then the estate is insolvent and the beneficiaries would not be able to receive any legacies. In this instance, as executor it would be sensible to employ a professional adviser to unravel the case, because creditors are paid in a strict order of priority in accordance with bankruptcy laws. The cost of these expenses would be paid for from the estate even before any beneficiary or creditor. This particular problem can throw out complications which are many and varied, one being that claims submitted may exceed the known sum owed.

Another complication can be the possibility of someone making a claim against the estate, seeking to gain a share or a larger share. Advice from your solicitor would be essential since either negotiations will need to take place to decide on the portion to be awarded (if the claimant does have a case) or because the claimant contesting the matter is taking the case to court.

These may all sound quite alarming but in the majority of cases matters are relatively straightforward with complexities rarely arising. Simple problems can be dealt with by asking the staff at the Personal Applications Department at the Probate Registry what the best course of action would be or whom you should go to.

The Probate Registry

The Probate Registry is part of the Family Division within the

High Court structure and as such comes within the Civil Court confines responsible for the Lord Chancellor's office. The Registry dates back to Norman times when Bishops Courts began to administer the wills of the deceased.

In 1357, the Courts were required by statute to pass on the administration of property from the Bishops Courts to the deceased's closest relative. In 1857, a further change took place when the District Probate Registries were introduced as a division within the Probate, Admiralty and Divorce Division of the High Court. In 1970 the Administration of Justice Act placed the probate section in the newly founded family division within the High Court, where it remains today.

The Probate Registry in England and Wales is unusual in that it provides people with advice and assistance which may be needed in order for them, as individuals, to obtain the grant of probate or letters of administration. In Scotland, the Commissary Court does give assistance but this is limited to small estates.

How can it help?

The Probate Registry is the linchpin of the proceedings. Its equivalent in Scotland is the Commissary Office.

The main function of the Registry is to give a grant of representation to the executor or next of kin. This grant is a document bearing the court seal, which states that the person named is authorised to deal with the estate. In fact, the document empowers that person to do anything which the deceased could have done if he were alive.

The Registry cannot advise you on making a will. It can, however, deal with any queries you may have in connection with making the will.

Probate Registries and Probate subRegistries are open daily during normal office hours. The probate administration system in England and Wales is a three-tiered one. There are eleven District Probate Registries in England and Wales and, of course, there is also Somerset House. The Registries also have subRegistries linked to them. There are also small Probate Offices which deal only with personal callers. These officers may be open for only one day a week or, in some cases, one day a month. Local Probate Offices are linked not only to Registries but to subRegistries as well.

All branches send out application forms, which start the whole proceedings, from their Personal Applications Department. Proceedings are straightforward, see page 89. A list of Registries, subRegistries and Offices are noted on pages 85–7.

Upon telephoning or writing to the Registry you will receive an envelope containing all the forms which are needed. The turn-round time for dealing with these is usually two or three weeks, although proceedings can be speeded up. The delay is not caused here but usually when the executor is trying to pull together all the details of the estate.

A probate fee is payable, starting at £1 for a net estate up to £500 and increasing thereafter, see Appendix 2 on page 127.

Once probate has been granted, executors can proceed to collect in and transfer monies to debtors and beneficiaries.

When neither a will nor a relative can be found the probate Treasury Solicitor will take over the duties. The Treasury Solicitor will make enquiries on behalf of the Crown to trace relatives. After considerable checking to see whether there are any living relatives with valid claims he will then declare none have been found, and only then does the Crown become entitled to the estate. (A valid claim can be made by,say, a common-law husband or wife, or close friends who helped the deceased over the years without payment, or creditors.)

There are three types of document issued by the Probate Registry, namely, Grant of Probate when there is a valid will with executors applying; Letters of Administration when there is a valid will but executors have not been appointed; or Letters of Administration given when there is no will.

There are three areas where Grant of Probate or Letters of Administration may not be needed.

1. If the property consists of cash (ie physical notes and coins), if the effects are household ones or a car, and provided there is no dispute between the immediate relatives as to the distribution.
2. If there is no more than £5000 held in savings accounts or in National Savings and pension funds it is possible that the sums may be released without the need for a grant. However, this is discretionary and the National Savings Bank may ask for a grant to be taken if it considers that circumstances require it.
3. Individual sums of money in banks and building societies do not exceed £5000. However, many of the banks make a charge for preparing documents and this charge is, in some cases, much more expensive than taking out the grant in the first instance.

Probate Registries and their local Probate Offices

Birmingham – 3rd Floor, Cavendish House, Waterloo Street, Birmingham B2 5PS. Tel 021-236 4560/6263.
Local Probate Offices – Coventry, Kidderminster, Lichfield, Northampton, Wolverhampton.

Brighton – William Street, Brighton BN2 2LG. Tel 0273 684071.
Local Probate Offices – Crawley, Hastings, Tunbridge Wells, Worthing.

Bristol – The Crescent Centre, Temple Back, Bristol BS1 6EP. Tel 0272 273915/24619.
Local Probate Offices – Bath, Taunton, Weston super Mare.

Ipswich – Level 3, Haven House, 17 Lower Brook Street, Ipswich IP4 1ON. Tel 0473 53724.
Local Probate Offices – Chelmsford, Colchester.

Leeds – Devereux House, East Parade, Leeds LS1 2BA. Tel 0532 431505.
Local Probate Offices – Bradford, Harrogate, Huddersfield.

Liverpool – 3rd Floor, India Buildings, Water Street, Liverpool L2 0QR. Tel 051-236 8264.
Local Probate Offices – Southport, St Helens, Wallasey.

Llandaff – Probate Registry of Wales, 49 Cardiff Road, Llandaff, Cardiff CF5 2YW. Tel 0222 562422.
Local Probate Offices – Bridgend, Newport, Pontypridd.

London – Principal Registry, Family Division of the High Court, 5th Floor, Golden Cross House, Duncannon Street, London WC2N 4JF. Tel 01-210 4595.
Local Probate Offices – Croydon, Enfield, Harlow, Kingston, Luton, Romford, Slough, Southend-on-Sea, Watford, Woolwich.

Manchester – 9th Floor, Astley House, 23 Quay Street, Manchester M3 4AT. Tel 061-834 4319.
Local Probate Offices – Bolton, Burnley, Oldham, Stockport, Warrington, Wigan.

Newcastle upon Tyne – 2nd Floor, Plummer House, Croft Street, Newcastle upon Tyne NE1 6ND. Tel 091-261 8383.
Local Probate Offices – Ashington, Sunderland.

Oxford – 10A New Road, Oxford OX1 1LY. Tel 0865 241163.
Local Probate Offices – Aylesbury, Banbury, High Wycombe, Reading, Swindon.

Winchester – 4th Floor, Cromwell House, Andover Road, Winchester SO23 7EW. Tel 0962 53046/63771.
Local Probate Offices – Basingstoke, Bournemouth, Dorchester, Guildford, Newport, Portsmouth, Salisbury, Southampton.

Probate subRegistries

Probate subRegistries can be found in the following towns:

Bangor – 1st Floor, Bron Castell, High Street, Bangor LL57 1YS. Tel 0248 362410.

Bodmin – Market Street, Bodmin PL31 2JW. Tel 0208 2279.
Local Probate Offices – Truro, Plymouth.

Carlisle – 2 Victoria Place, Carlisle CA1 1ER. Tel 228 21751.
Local Probate Office – Workington.

Carmarthen – 14 King Street, Carmarthen, Dyfed SA31 1BL. Tel 0267 236238.
Local Probate Offices – Aberystwyth, Haverfordwest, Swansea.

Chester – 5th Floor, Hamilton House, Hamilton Place, Chester CH1 2DA. Tel 0244 45082.
Local Probate Offices – Rhyl, Wrexham.

Exeter – Eastgate House, High Street, Exeter EX4 3JZ. Tel 0392 74515.
Local Probate Offices – Barnstaple, Newton Abbot, Yeovil.

Gloucester – 3 Pitt Street, Gloucester GL1 2JB. Tel 0452 22585.
Local Probate Offices – Cheltenham, Hereford, Worcester.

Lancaster – Mitre House, Church Street, Lancaster LA1 1HE. Tel 0524 36625.
Local Probate Offices – Barrow in Furness, Blackpool, Preston.

Leicester – Government Buildings, Newark Street, Leicester LE1 5SE. Tel 0533 546117.
Local Probate Offices – Bedford, Kettering.

Lincoln – Mill House, Brayford Side North, Lincoln LN1 1YW. Tel 0522 23648.
Local Probate Office – Grimsby.

Maidstone – The Law Courts, Barker Road, Maidstone ME19 8EW. Tel 0622 54966.
Local Probate Offices – Canterbury, Chatham, Folkestone.

Middlesbrough – 12/16 Woodlands Road, Middlesbrough TS1 3BS. Tel 0642 244770.
Local Probate Offices – Darlington, Durham.

Norwich – 65 Cathedral Close, Norwich NR1 4DN. Tel 0603 626648/623839.
Local Probate Office – Lowestoft.

Nottingham – Upper Ground Floor, Lambert House, Talbot Street, Nottingham NG1 5NR. Tel 0602 414288.
Local Probate Offices – Derby, Mansfield.

Peterborough – Clifton House, Broadway, Peterborough PE1 1SL. Tel 0733 62802.
Local Probate Offices – Cambridge, Kings Lynn.

Sheffield – 4th Floor, Belgrave House, Bank Street, Sheffield S1 1QN. Tel 0742 75317/729920.
Local Probate Offices – Chesterfield, Doncaster.

Stoke on Trent – 2nd Floor, Town Hall, Albion Street, Hanley, Stoke on Trent ST1 1QL. Tel 0782 23736.
Local Probate Offices – Crewe, Shrewsbury, Stafford.

York – Duncombe Place, York YO1 2EA. Tel 0904 24210.
Local Probate Offices – Hull, Scarborough.

Where else can advice be sought?

The time to get in touch with your tax consultant should be before you start to make out your will. Like the solicitor, the consultant will charge a fee for his time. But remember, not all accountants have estate planning experience and you need to check carefully that your chosen consultant does. Ask your solicitor if he can recommend someone. Here again, ask how much the consultant is likely to charge.

Your bank will also be able to offer help. Banks too charge a fee for dealing with probate matters and that charge can be steep, up to 5 per cent of the estate's value and a withdrawal fee as well. Banks will also keep your will.

If it is necessary to have a bank account for the estate (known as a *executorship account*) remember to ask the bank what charge, if any, will be levied. Usually a bank charges a fee for administration – deducted from the account. But because of increased competition not only between banks but between building societies as well, charges and services are constantly changing. With some building societies now offering a banking service it would be worthwhile to shop around for free banking.

Another organisation which can help is the Citizens Advice Bureaux. This organisation has the advantage of having offices in all the major towns and cities throughout the United Kingdom. If one centre does not have the information it can refer to a larger centre or recommend whom to go to.

When valuing the estate you may need to gain valuations from different sources, depending on the estate's assets. For example, you may need to approach estate agents for property valuation, antique dealers for furniture, jewellers for jewellery and so on. Do ask if the valuation is free, otherwise you might find the estate faced with a bill. In addition to these 'property' valuations you will have to write to organisations such as banks and insurance companies, asking for a valuation of accounts or insurance policies. You might have to write to a publisher to ask for the current amount due on the royalties from a book; the list of contacts goes on, depending on the nature of the estate's assets.

9

DOCUMENTATION

Death certificate

An executor's duties start with the death of the testator. One of the first duties may be to register the death and collect the death certificate. When doing this at the Registry for Births, Deaths and Marriages, a form PA2, entitled *How to obtain probate* may be given to you. If not, then ask for a copy. Basically, the booklet tells you how to proceed with probate, who can apply for the grant and where to apply.

The simplest way of receiving all the relevant forms is to telephone your nearest Probate Registry (or subRegistry) and ask for the forms to be sent to you. (For a full list of Probate offices see pages 85–7.) The forms you will receive not only include the probate form but also tax declaration forms which will eventually be sent off to the Capital Taxes Office.

Depending upon the circumstances of the death, an initial medical death certificate is usually issued by the hospital authorities or the General Practitioner in attendance where death occurs at home. In the case of sudden death, this is only issued once the autopsy has been carried out. The certificate, given to the closest relative or known executor, has to be sent or taken to the Registrar of Births, Deaths and Marriages within five days. That Registrar will then issue the formal death certificate.

It is advisable to obtain extra copies of the death certificate which can be purchased at the time the original one is given, as you will need to send a copy to each company where assets are held.

It is unfortunate, but there are occasions when death occurs while abroad causing added strain on the next of kin. The first thing to do is to register the death with the appropriate authority in the country where the death occurred. A death certificate should also be obtained. The British embassy or consulate in that country can help with arrangements in bringing the body or ashes back to the United Kingdom, and you can also register the death with them.

Unless you are insured for such eventualities, the cost of bringing the body back to this country has to be borne by yourself and the cost can be high. The embassy or consulate can help with a small interim loan to facilitate this wish but it will only cover a tiny portion of the overall cost.

What is a grant and why is it necessary?

A grant is in effect a court order. It is your legal proof of title to deal with the estate. Without it some companies and banks will not release money or assets held in the deceased's name. The grant allows that these assets are passed on to the named person to deal with.

A grant may not be necessary in certain cases, for example, if a house was jointly owned. But if the couple still had a mortgage it would be advisable to check with the building society to see if the deeds were in order.

As a simple rule of thumb you will amost certainly need a grant if the property is solely owned by the deceased in his or her name or if the estate exceeds £5000.

After contacting the Probate Registry you will receive a deluge of forms. The following section explains what these are.

What are all these forms for?

Form Cap 40 is a tax form for detailing any stocks, shares, unit trusts, etc. On it you must list for each holding the company name of each company's shares held by the deceased along with the type of shares, or in the case of stocks or unit trusts the unit of quotation. In column 2 the exact number of shares or the total amount of stock has to be inserted and the market price at the 'date of valuation', in other words at the date of death. To value these holdings, obtain a copy of any of national newspapers or visit your local library and ask to see a copy of the *Stock Registry*. To find the figures for the previous day's trading look at a newspaper printed on the day following the death as the figures are printed the morning after the close of trading. Therefore the figure on shares, unit trusts etc for, say, Monday 27 September would be printed in the Tuesday 28 September edition. If there are no assets the form can be left blank.

Form Cap 37 is another tax form and refers to any house, land or property owned by the deceased. All such property owned must be noted separately with a full description and the type of tenure, ie freehold or leasehold. If the property has been let then full details need to be inserted in column 4. Any agricultural use (including timber or grazing) must also be noted and inserted in column 5. In the last column a gross value has to be inserted. If you feel able you may estimate the figure on the basis of other like properties being sold in the area. Otherwise contact an estate agent and ask for a free valuation. Most estate agents now give a free valuation but it is worth asking before issuing instructions. If the house is to be sold then your estimate will be accepted initially because the actual value for tax will be the sale value.

If the property is mixed, that is part of it is set aside for orchards, grazing, buildings and so on, then you have to state where the boundary for each is. It is suggested that if the plot is large enough to note the ordnance survey reference alongside a roughly drawn plan of the local.

Again, if the form is not applicable it should be left blank.

Form Cap 44 is a tax return for the entire estate, including securities and property already noted in detail in Cap 37 and 40. This is a straightforward form asking for all assets including household and personal goods to have a gross value placed against each. The officials are well aware that the second-hand value of personal goods is likely to be low. This form also asks for any known debts, such as mortgages, funeral expenses and so on to be listed. Although the form is a long one you need only fill in those parts which apply.

Finally, after all these tax forms, the last form relates to the grant of probate itself. Form PR83 asks the basic questions such as the deceased's name, address, age, family connections, whether there is a will and so forth.

Details of the forms sent out by the Commissary Office in Scotland or by the Capital Taxes office are found in Chapter 11.

WHAT HAPPENS NEXT?
Once these forms have been completed they should be returned along with the death certificate and original will to the Personal

Applications Department of the Probate Registry. It is advisable for you to keep for your records a photocopy of each.

Once the staff at the Probate Registry have had a chance to look at these forms you will be invited to attend a meeting at the nearest office to confirm the accuracy of the information supplied. Usually only one visit is necessary. Once this is over and any tax due has been paid then a grant of probate is issued.

Of course, depending upon the complexities of the estate the time taken to complete these forms will vary. You may find a considerable amount of time has elapsed between asking for the forms and returning them as in the meantime you have had to assess the estate and value its assets.

A grant will not be issued if there is any objection registered in respect of the estate and will only be actioned once it has been resolved. If the objections cannot be resolved then in all probability the matter will be referred to a judge in the Chancery Division of the courts. However, before that the objection may be heard at the District Probate Registry to ascertain if there are any valid points. Just a word of comfort – these problems rarely arise.

Again, if you have any doubts about whether or not your application is suitable for a personal application, speak to the Probate Registry staff.

10

VALUING AND ADMINISTERING THE ESTATE

The example of a will shown on pages 47–9 will be referred to in this chapter to take you, as an executor, through the different jobs which have to be done when valuing and administering a will. The only variation to this will, of course, is that you are seen as the executor.

As an executor you will know where Edith's will is located; also general instructions, such as her wish to be buried in the local church's graveyard. Edith's estate is provisionally valued at £190,000 but part of it has been left to her husband, James. As there is no mortgage on the farm – only on the house – once inheritance tax on the estate has been paid and debts settled it can pass to Richard. Any running costs incurred during this time can be settled by the estate, see Chapter 7 for tax considerations. As a rule of thumb, however, remember that tax is payable by the individual beneficiary (unless stated to the contrary in the will) in direct proportion to the value of the gift which is in relation to the total taxable estate.

The same principle applies to a loan secured against an asset which forms part of the estate. For example, should Edith have taken out an overdraft before her death with her portfolio of shares as security against the loan, when Richard inherited the shares he would have to settle the overdraft unless Edith had stated in her will that the overdraft was to be repaid by the remainder of her estate. If Edith had left half of the portfolio to Richard and the other half to James both would have to settle the debt in direct proportion to the value of their individual inheritance. Moreover, if Edith had intended to give the assets freely without any liability than unless she made those wishes clear in her will her beneficiaries would have to repay any debts secured against the gifts noted in the will.

It is best to obtain a number of copies of a death certificate from the Births, Deaths and Marriages Registrar. As executor you will have a rough idea of how many certificates are required as a copy should be sent to each organisation holding Edith's assets.

Armed with these copies, you can now send letters to Edith's bank, building society, National Savings, indeed, all organisations involved. In the letter you must explain that you are the executor and that you are in the process of applying for a grant of probate. Proof of the death in the form of the death certificate should be enclosed. Request a statement of account, including interest if applicable, up to the date of death. Although not necessary if joint accounts are held, if Edith had been a single person you would have to ask the bank or building society to freeze the debits and credits going in to and out of her accounts. All queries should then be forwarded to you.

Another incidental job often overlooked is the redirection of post. You should arrange for a redirection of Edith's post for either three, six or 12 months. As the precise length of time of your executorial duties is not known it is best to arrange redirection for 12 months.

How to start

Before the forms arrive you should start to make a list of all Edith's assets based on information to hand and also that information noted in her will. Against each item you note an estimate of its value. For some of these assets this may prove difficult and so help should be sought from the appropriate source. For example, Edith had a sizeable stamp collection. Stamps are notoriously difficult to value and expert advice should be sought from a philately society or by approaching an organisation such as Stanley Gibbons who deals in stamps. Written valuations should always be asked for.

With these valuations to hand you can now start to prepare a more detailed inventory of Edith's estate.

Property

Although not essential, it is important to get a professional valuation on property unless you are able, on the basis of other properties nearby and recently sold, to make your own valuation. The Inland Revenue may, after the grant has been issued, decide to send round its own official, the District Valuer. He will value the property based on his own opinion of the current market price, which might differ from that considered by the estate agent to be realistic. If you do a valuation through an estate agent you can put the lower of the two prices down since, if the District Valuer thinks that it is too low, he can amend it upward, but if you put the higher of the two values down you are stuck with it as chances are that he will not reduce the amount.

The District Valuer does not have time to come round and inspect all properties that form part of estates. But he will almost certainly do so if a clearly inaccurate low valuation is given.

If a house is to be sold your own estimate will serve instead of one from an estate agent. This is because the actual value of the realised price will have to be notified to the Revenue after the sale.

Of course, in Edith's case the house was jointly owned and her share automatically passes to her husband upon her death. However, for inheritance tax purposes her share still has to be valued. So if the house's value was £100,000 her share of it would be £50,000. The same applies to a mortgage. If the mortgage was £40,000 her share would be seen as £20,000 and that amount would be deducted from her share of the house. For other relationships, however, the actual proportion of monies provided for purchase is applied to the present day value. Whoever held the mortgage to the property would have to be informed and an exact figure requested as to the outstanding mortgage at the date of death.

By value, the tax authority means the price that the property could be sold for if it were put on the open market with vacant possession on the day that Edith died. If the house were tenanted then a lower value is given to take account of this restriction.

If you were not sure whether the property was held jointly, an examination of the title deeds would be necessary.

Example 1. How to calculate inheritance tax
(for ease of calculation the figures refer to the following table)

		£
Total value of estate		190,000
Less		
Funeral expenses	1,250	
Half share of mortgage	20,000	
	21,250	168,750

Less current allowable level of inheritance tax		110,000
Total taxable estate		58,750
Inheritance tax at 40% =	£23,500	

Example 2. Inventory and valuation of Edith Baker's estate

Details	Approximate value £
Somerset Farm	75,000
Broadwood (value £100,000) half share	50,000
Jewellery:	
diamond and emerald brooch	650
engagement ring and wedding ring	400
other jewellery	600
Antiques:	
grandmother clock	1,500
chaise longue	1,000
four-poster bed	1,000
2 Victorian button-back chairs	400
1 painting, early 19th century	1,000
Investments:	
National Savings certificates	5,000
Building society account (1)	3,000
(account no 0000000)	
Building society account (2)	2,000
(account no 111111)	
premium bonds	500
stocks and shares (see separate list)	15,000
Insurance:	
endowment policy (no 000002)	10,500
(with profits, to be verified)	
Life insurance policy (no 000332)	20,000
Other miscellaneous items	2,450
Total of estate	190,000

Debts	£
Funeral expenses	1,250
Miscellaneous expenses	1,000
Half share of mortgage on Broadwood	20,000
Total liabilities	22,250

Less	
Probate fee	150
Inheritance tax	23,500

Approximate value for distribution	£144,100

Example 3. Letter requesting details on the estate's behalf

The following is a sample letter which should be sent out to each organisation holding estate assets.

---

12 Calthorpe Lane,
Bearwood,
Warwickshire BR2 2PJ

16th June 1989

The Manager
Birmingham Building Society
2B High Street
Birmingham B2 2RT

Dear Sir

I am the executor of the will of the late Edith Mary Baker of Broadwood, Non-Such Lane, Burton, Warwickshire who died on   day — of   19xx. I am writing to request the following information as to the exact value of Mrs Baker's assets held in her name with your organisation. If there are any details missing please supply them.

Account number:
Type of account:
Date of account opened:
Value of account at date of death:
Interest accrued up to date of death:
Interest accrued since death up to the date of letter:
Has tax been deducted?
If so, what amount of tax:
Since death, has tax been deducted?
    If so, what amount of tax:

I enclose a copy of Edith Baker's death certificate.

Would you please notify me of any formalities needed before you release the money to me.

My address is as shown at the top of this letter.

Yours faithfully,

J G Person

The first valuation hurdle is over. Edith's estate is clearly solvent with her assets exceeding any liabilities. All legacies can therefore be met in full.

Now you would have to enquire whether Edith was a beneficiary of a trust or life interest from any of her ancestors or other persons' estates. If she had been then exact details of the inheritance would have to be obtained. For this example, Edith was not a beneficiary of a trust or life interest.

The Inland Revenue normally require the precise value of items from pensions, life and endowment policies to building society accounts. But if it is clear that the estate is a small one then approximate valuations are accepted by the Probate Registry.

Based on the response from each organisation which you have written to, once probate has been granted a copy of the official grant should be sent to each company for their records. All copy letters either sent to you or received by you should be kept on file.

National Savings Certificates

As Edith had bought National Savings certificates you would need to obtain a claims form from your local post office. This is then filled in and sent to the address printed on the back of the leaflet. In this example, as Edith did not have much money in National Savings, you can ask for this to be repaid. Each certificate number has to be noted on the form with its individual value and number of units. Also needed is the certificate's serial number and the date of issue.

Premium Bonds

When assessing Edith's premium bonds, if you are uncertain whether you have, in fact, got all the bond certificates then you should write in the first instance to the Bonds and Stock Office at Lytham St Annes, Lancs FYO 1YN (Tel: 0253 721212).

As premium bonds have a face value with no interest being paid they do not need an official valuation merely the number held totalled up.

Premium bonds cannot be transferred to beneficiaries. The same is true for National Savings. Nor will the Bonds and Stock Office pay out any money to the estate without receiving the grant of probate. Of course, if savings are held jointly this problem does not arise as the surviving joint holder can request payment on the production of the death certificate.

It is best to leave the premium bonds *in situ* until the final stage, just before distribution. But you must advise the Bonds and Stock Office of your address and your role as executor. Should a bond win within one year of the death, then the cheque can be sent to you on behalf of the estate once probate has been granted. The money received goes directly into the executorship account for the beneficiaries.

Insurance

You should also inform the insurance companies involved of Edith's death and stop any direct debit payments currently being made to them. As Edith had a straight life policy the company should pay out for the sum insured on proof of death, although the immediate payment depends on the value of the policy.

Edith's life insurance and endowment policies had been taken out a long time ago. The endowment policy was 'with profits' which means that in addition to the paid-up value shown on the policy there is an additional 'bonus' sum to be paid. This additional amount depends on how well the insurance company's managers have done with their investments. In your letter to the insurance company you should not only give the policy numbers but also the actual value of the policies and dates of issue. In the case of the endowment policy you should ask what the 'with profits' value is.

Edith had not invested in a pension nor had she a company pension. Again, if she had you would have to write to the company concerned notifying them of her death and asking for a precise valuation.

Bank and building society accounts

As James and Edith had held a joint deposit and current account you would not need to amend any normal payments that go through as a matter of course. Joint account holders can continue to withdraw from a jointly held account. However, for inheritance tax purposes you have to obtain a balance of each account at the date of death. That amount is usually halved, in the case of accounts held jointly by husband and wife, and the proportion provided by the deceased will be put down on the Capital Taxes form. Accounts held by a single person would have to be noted at full value and payment into and out of these accounts would have to be stopped.

You should now be receiving payments (and bills). It might be worthwhile to open an executorship account at this stage. Do ask the bank what charges are likely to apply. (This charge is deducted from the residue of the estate.) Check with both banks and building societies where Edith held an account to see whether there is a second or third account not known to you. When visiting either organisation return any bank cards or passbooks held, obtaining a receipt for each.

Shares and other investments

For a number of years Edith had dabbled on the stock market and had a variety of shares in her portfolio. You would have to locate the share certificates and on a separate sheet note the number and type of shares held and the names of each company found on individual certificates. (The same would apply for like investments, ie unit trusts, PEPs.) Obtain the *Financial Times* (or any of the major national daily papers) dated the day after Edith's death, and you should find buying and selling prices quoted. The value you are looking at is the lower of the two quoted, as you buy at a higher price and sell at a lower one. You value the shares by taking the lower of the two figures quoted in the *Stock Register* and adding one-quarter of the difference between the share's two prices. You can also value shares by subtracting the bid from the offer price and taking half of that figure and adding it to the lower of the quoted prices. These figures can be found in other publications, for example the Stock Exchange publish the *Daily Official List* and main libraries hold a copy of the *Stock Register*.

If the death occurs over a weekend, you can choose to value shares either on the basis of Friday's closing price or Monday's closing value. The lower price will, of course, result in less tax and possibly lower probate fees.

Of course, if you are unhappy about valuing shares yourself,

Example 4. Share value list

Amount of shares held	Company	Price quoted	Value of holding
500	BW Ordinary	156/150	£757.50
600	KP Ordinary	172/160	£978
600	Plate & Co	148/140	£852
1000	Copper Works	222/210	£2,130
800	Lampshade Ltd	170/163	£1,330

(*Note:* The names and prices above are examples only and do not relate to any known company.)

you can ask the securities department of your bank to do this. Alternatively, telephone the stockbroker who sold the shares in the first place.

Most shares are quoted in pence. For instance, a value quoted at, say, 578 translates into £5 and 78 pence. Certain high value shares, however, are quoted in pounds.

You may notice from the certificates that dividend payments are made twice yearly. To find out whether any payment is due write to the company secretary of each company concerned and ask whether any dividends are due. If you do not have the head office address of each company then contact the Stock Exchange, as all quoted companies are registered there with their head office addresses noted on file.

When checking the newspaper, you might have noticed that beside the quoted price a symbol or letters are shown. 'Xd' means that the price quoted excludes the dividend value. Usually, this is noted some two weeks or so before the dividend is due. So if Edith had sold the shares with the xd in force then she would still receive the dividend on those shares and not the person who bought them. The price quoted is, therefore, lower to take this into account.

Dividend cheques are usually sent out on the day the dividend is due but prepared beforehand.

If a rights issue had been in force it would mean that the company is issuing new shares to existing shareholders at a price lower than the current market price. In this instance a letter is sent out to all shareholders and the proportion of shares offered is based on the number of existing shares held.

A scrip issue would be noted alongside the price. Exscrip means that it is the value placed on the share while the company is issuing new shares to existing shareholders based on the percentage of their existing holding.

Edith's portfolio had not included any unit trusts. If it had you would have to write to the unit trust companies concerned. Unlike shares, where you hold a number of shares in a particular company, for a unit trust you hold units within a trust and that trust has a specified category of investment, say, Small Company, Far East, Recovery and so on. Basically, money put into a unit trust is 'pooled', with other investors' money in the same category of trust, to purchase shares in companies fulfilling that category's definition.

Other income

As she had not worked for many years, Edith had no income coming in other than the occasional dividend payment and interest from her building society accounts, deposit accounts and National Savings. You would still have to write to the Inspector of Taxes at the nearest Inland Revenue office notifying the Revenue of her death and letting them know that the small amounts of income earned had already been noted on James's income tax return form.

Had Edith been a pensioner then her state pension allowance book would have to be returned to the nearest Department of Social Security office, whose address can be found in the telephone directory.

Hire purchase

Should a hire purchase agreement have been in force then you would have to write to the company concerned and ask for an exact assessment of the debt. In the meantime, if the agreement had been jointly signed, the surviving partner could continue to pay the monthly instalments.

Listing the valuations

Most of the contents of the house had been jointly owned with no hire purchase scheme, therefore it would be a matter of listing all items and placing an approximate second-hand value against each. A family car, for instance, valued at £1000 would be apportioned to her estate at £500, in other words half the value. As the jewellery had already been itemised in her will this need not be done but the full valuation would have to be placed on the valuation sheet as Edith owned the jewellery outright. General items, such as clothes, tables, chairs, TV and so on, would not need itemising but, again, a second-hand value would have to be noted. The Inland Revenue do not expect an exact and absolute value for these items down to the last pound but do expect a valuation that is sensible and realistic. Again, these general items, if jointly owned, have half of each value listed.

Any cash in Edith's possession at the time of her death, whether in her handbag or in her desk drawer at home, would have to be accounted for on the valuation sheet. This loose cash could be used on the estate's behalf to purchase stamps, for example, provided it is accounted for. Any money spend personally on the funeral could be reimbursed from the estate once probate has been granted.

Let us assume that the estate, once valued, exceeds the first valuation figure. As this is only your rough guide it would not matter. What does matter, however, is that the value on the Capital Taxes form is correct.

With all the valuations to hand, the forms can be completed and despatched to the Probate Registry. In the meantime you should continue to administer the estate, collecting the debt, noting any assets that have been redeemed and keeping close account of all transactions in your own bookkeeping journal.

11

WHAT HAPPENS IN SCOTLAND?

In most cases you will have had prior notice of your task as executor. However, it is worth noting at the outset that in Scotland, except where an estate does not exceed £13,000 gross and is known as a small estate (see below), in the majority of cases a solicitor's service is used. This chapter, therefore, briefly notes procedures in Scotland, explaining the different terminology used and highlights areas of major differences.

The first thing to do, wherever you live in the United Kingdom, after the death is to find the will. It may have been lodged with the deceased's bank, solicitor or hidden away at the family home. Although a photocopy of a will cannot be substituted for the original – except for an action of declaration brought in the Court of Session – it is advisable to have a photocopy for your own reference.

What is a 'small estate'?

In Scotland a special procedure is followed if an estate is under £13,000 gross. The legal term for this size of estate is a *small estate*. For estates which exceed this value then this involves, in intestate cases, a petition to the court for appointment of an *'executor-dative'*. Presentation (inventory of estate and petition) is rarely made by personal application; instead, it is presented by a solicitor.

The staff at the Commissary Offices throughout Scotland will process small estates provided that complications do not arise. If they are able to assist then they require full and detailed information regarding the estate and its assets. In calculating the value of the estate, debts such as funeral expenses, gas or electricity bills, hire purchase payments, outstanding mortgage must be disregarded. The applicant must supply information to the staff at the Commissary Office making a list and supporting this list by documentation. All property must be included in this list, even accounts held jointly.

In addition to a list of assets, you would also have to supply a death certificate, marriage certificate if the surviving spouse is applying to be the executor, a divorce certificate, if applicable, and a will. If there is no will the court will appoint the closest relative in order of 'preferred' status, namely spouse, child, brother or sister, parent.

As in England, there is no charge made by the Sheriff Clerk in giving advice or information or for completing the inventory or forms on an applicant's behalf. Again as in England, there is a statutory fee charged whether a solicitor is used or not and this is calculated on the basis of the gross value of the estate. For an estate of £3000 or under no fee is charged and between £3001 and £13,000 the fee is £20.

If there is a surviving spouse and you apply on his or her behalf then you will be asked to obtain a *bond of caution* (type of insurance policy against any mistakes or appropriation of the funds) from an insurance company, before you are able to take on the task.

INFORMATION NEEDED

Bank and building society accounts
The passbooks must be presented to the companies for updating. Any interest incurred up to the date of death must be noted by the manager in pencil. If you cannot find a passbook then write to the bank or building society concerned and ask them to supply you with a letter stating the type of account, the account number and the value plus interest, noted separately.

Insurance policies
The insurance company must be asked to supply details of the policy, its value, its number and any bonuses applicable.

National Savings Bank (including National Savings Certificates and Grannie Bonds)
A letter must be obtained from the Director of Savings giving the value of each holding, including interest, up to the date of death. This address will be found on the reverse of the claim form which

you obtain from your local post office. (Bonds and Stock Office, Blackpool, Lancs FY0 1BR.)

Premium Bonds
If the actual bonds cannot be produced then the holder's registration number should be given. if this also cannot be found, then write to the address found on page 98 and ask for confirmation of the numbers, stating why you need them.

Stocks and shares
The valuation route as found on page 100 needs to be followed and should include the value of the item, plus dividends. If a stockbroker or bank is used ask them to confirm these details in writing.

Heritable property
This includes a house, shop, land etc. A valuation from an estate agent, solicitor or other appropriate person must be obtained, again in writing. It is advisable, where heritable property forms part of an estate, for a solicitor's services to be used.

Rights

There are two rights given; first, prior rights and, second, legal rights. Prior rights means just that – the spouse or child has a right to the property and these rights must be satisfied before legal rights; legal rights allow for what is legally available to a spouse or descendant; see page 110 for further clarification.

Once you are sure that all the information and its supportive evidence is to hand then you need to arrange an interview with the Commissary Office. At the end of the interview some offices require that you depone (swear) an oath that the information given by you is 'full and true'. If the deceased died intestate, then you would need to bring two witnesses to the interview to swear on your behalf that you are who you say you are and that your relationship to the deceased is as you say. One witness must not be related to either the deceased or the applicant and the other witness, although a relative is allowable, must not be a beneficiary.

TAX FORMS
There are four tax forms in Scotland which need to be filled in along with an inventory of estate (Form X-1).

Form Cap 83 (1981) is an Inland Revenue Scotland form for small estates. On page 2 of the form the applicant has to swear that the information given is full and true. The same applies on Form B4 (1983) for excepted estates.

Lastly, there are forms Cap A3 for inheritance tax purposes sent with its own instruction booklet and Cap D-1 (1977) is for corrective or additional inventory belonging to the estate.

ESTATE CHECKLIST

An estate checklist, reproduced by courtesy of the Commissary Office in Edinburgh, is shown below. Indeed, this list could be used as a guide for those preparing an inventory of an estate in England, Wales or Northern Ireland. It is stressed, however, that this list is not exhaustive, merely an indication of how detailed the inventory should be. Details of each item, along with its current value at date of death, should accompany the list.

Bank and building society accounts including Post Office Giro
Insurance policies
Premium Bonds
Savings Bonds
National Savings Certificates
Old age pension
Invalidity pension
DSS death grant
Pension from employer
Holiday outstanding
Salary outstanding
Employer's death grant (gratuity)
Employer's superannuation
Mobility allowance
Shares, including those in co-operatives
Stocks (ie Treasury Stock, consolidated and public stock)
Bond and disposition in securities
Repayment of TV licence stamps
Overpayment of rent, rates (including rebates)
Gift vouchers
Estate abroad
Trust estate
Income from a trust
Rents from property
Beneficiary under a will
Personal effects

Motor car
Cash in hand (including in hospital, nursing home, etc)
Income tax repayment
Royalities
Repayment of club subscription (and motoring organisations)
Repayment of loans to clubs
House, garage
Business
Strip of land

What does it all mean?

It is important to understand what is meant by certain legal words and phrases as some of these differ between Scotland and England. For example, in Scotland, what is meant by 'the house' or 'the furnishings'? The house is the main or only abode of the deceased where he or she resided with his or her spouse and was in residence at the date of death. Furnishings mean any item of furniture owned by the deceased not including cars, jewellery or money. Cash has the same definition as in England, in other words any money held in a bank or building society or accounts where the money is kept as cash.

Should a will have been written appointing you as an executor you would be referred to as an *'executor nominate'*. As in England, if you find that you cannot fulfil your appointment for one reason or another you would have to sign a statement officially declining your role. You might be the only executor and, if so, you may ask another person to act as executor before resigning from your office.

In Scotland, if a person dies without a will then the court appoints an executor known as an *'executor dative'*. Just as in England, the duty of an executor dative is to collect, administer and distribute the assets according to the intestacy laws.

There are two types of estate: heritable (meaning house, buildings, land) and moveable (meaning furniture, cash etc). An estate usually has both as the majority of people now own their own home.

The final value of a house is determined once any outstanding debts, ie mortgage or home improvement loan, have been paid. If the deceased has died intestate then the value of the house up to £65,000 goes to the surviving spouse. Before 1 May 1988 the figure of £50,000 applied and it still does for deaths before that date.

If a house has no common ownership, in other words with a surviving spouse, child, but instead has a survivorship destination clause in the title deeds, then whoever is the survivor of this clause inherits the property, see below.

Children

In 1986 the Law Reform (Parent and Child) Scotland Act was passed. Before this Act a child born out of a marriage and not mentioned specially in the will could not inherit from his parents if the beneficiaries of the will were referred to as 'my children'. The illegitmate child could only claim legal rights. The 1986 Act applies only to wills signed after 26 March 1986.

The legal application of the word 'child' or 'children' in Scotland refers to children of a marriage, adopted children and now illegitimate children *but not* step children. For step children to be included in distribution of an estate the will has specifically to state the legacy.

A boy under the age of 14 and a girl under the age of 12 cannot legally accept a legacy themselves. Instead, the legacy has to be given to the parents or guardians on the child's behalf for the purpose of investing. The parents or guardians would have to sign the receipt for the legacy.

Once the children have reached the age of majority they would be able to receive the entire legacy including any interest earned.

Jointly owned property

If a property is owned jointly by two people then despite what is written in the will the house will automatically pass to the surviving owner as stated in the 'destination' clause in the property's title deeds. However, this does not apply if the destination has been recalled by the deceased in his lifetime. If the survivor is a beneficiary under the will and wishes to transfer the house to his name then this can be done by signing a document appropriately called a 'docket'. A solicitor will have to draw one up for you.

A docket contains the name(s) of the executor(s), the name of the deceased, and the name of the person to whom the property is being transferred. It has also to state what rights are involved, ie whether he or she has prior rights or legal rights to the property and whether it is part of the gift as noted in the will. The full address of the house must also be included. If the house is going to be sold then a document called a 'disposition' will have to be prepared, again by a solicitor.

Intestacy estate

Before 1964 the intestacy rules regarding the distribution to the surviving spouse and children were somewhat unfair. However, in 1964, the Succession (Scotland) Act effectively altered the existing intestacy rules.

Where there is a surviving spouse then by right he or she is entitled to be the sole executor of the estate. If the estate exceeds the prior rights then other entitled persons may act.

There are two further terms, already mentioned, peculiar to Scottish law, 'prior rights' and 'legal rights'. 'Prior rights' means that the surviving spouse has a 'right' to the deceased's house worth £65,000, furnishings worth £12,000 (excluding the car) and moveables worth £35,000. If there are children of the marriage then the extent of the right to moveables is limited to £21,000. But if there are no surviving descendants the cash value goes up to £35,000.

After prior rights have been satisfied then 'legal rights' apply. Legal rights are taken from that part of the estate which remains after debts and prior rights have been paid.

In Scotland, even with a will, you cannot absolutely exclude your spouse or children from inheriting part of your moveable estate, as they have a 'legal right' to part of it. If a spouse and children survive then the spouse takes half. If there is no surviving spouse then the children take half. Only the remaining one-third or one-half of the estate may be disposed of by the testator. However, the heritable estate may be disposed of as the testator wishes.

The estate that remains after both prior rights and legal rights have been satisfied is known as 'free estate'. This portion is distributed according to the laws of intestate succession to the children or to other relatives of the deceased.

If there is an outstanding balance on the mortgage then the surviving spouse receives the value of the house less any outstanding mortgage. This is so even if an endowment policy formed part of the estate to pay off the mortgage upon death.

Where the furnishings of the house exceed £12,000, the surviving spouse is entitled to choose furnishings up to value of £12,000. Again, the value received is limited to the value in the estate.

Note: A car, jewellery or money is not included in the term furnishings and furnishings do not necessarily have to be located in the deceased person's home.

Where there is no surviving spouse, the children inherit. If there are no surviving children then other descendants inherit the estate. The order of succession after spouse and children is: (1) parents: (2) brothers and sisters and their descendants; (3) uncles, aunts and their descendants; (4) other living traceable descendants until someone is found. The estate is equally divided between .surviving descendants. Despite extensive searches by the executor dative, if no relative can be traced the estate goes to the Crown once all expenses and debts have been paid.

Does divorce alter a will?

Unlike England, where if a person makes out a will and then marries and subsequently divorces the granting of the 'decree absolute' will make the will invalid, in Scotland this does not apply. Neither marriage nor divorce invalidates a will.

An interesting point arises from this. If you do not make out a new will setting aside gifts or money to your new spouse, she will not benefit under this old will. There is a way around this, however. The new spouse can claim legal rights which would entitle her to one-third but of the moveable estate only. She could not claim the house.

Debts

There are three categories of debt in Scotland: 'secured debts' (ie overdraft, mortgage), 'privileged debts' (funeral expenses, rates), and 'ordinary debts' (butcher, baker and candlestick maker). You can only secure debts and privileged debts as and when the money is available, but ordinary debts have to wait until the estate is finalised, usually six months after the date of death.

For the purpose of division of the estate, debts can only be applied to its equivalent source of estate. In other words a loan against the house (heritable) can only be set against that source. Similarly, expenses such as telephone bills and funeral expenses must be paid out of the moveable estate.

This is where matters start to get complicated. Calculating the net moveable estate or heritable property and working out the legal rights and so on. It is, therefore, not within the scope of this book to elucidate further and you would be well advised to involve a solicitor.

Useful addresses

Payment of stamp duty
Controller of Stamps (Scotland)
16 Picardy Place
Edinburgh EH1 3AB

Registrar of Deeds
Registers of Scotland
Meadowbank House
London Road
Edinburgh EH8 7AU

HM Commissary Office
16 North Bank Street
Edinburgh EH1 2NJ

Supplier of inheritance tax inventory forms
Capital Taxes Office
16 Picardy Place
Edinburgh EH1 3AB

Forms can also be obtained from Sheriff Courts and main post offices throughout Scotland.

12

WINDING UP AN ESTATE

The first thing that usually crosses an executor's mind is the release of the house. As more and more people have now purchased their own home this usually means that there is a mortgage to consider. For mortgages which are linked to insurance policies the amount outstanding on death is automatically paid off.

Property

The first thing that has to be looked at is the title of the house. If it is in joint ownership then it merely passes on to the survivor. However, if the house is going to a named beneficiary then, in certain instances, the building society may agree for that person to take over the existing mortgage or to remortgage the house.

If there are not sufficient assets for distribution you might have to put the house up for sale. Once it has been sold and the mortgage paid off then the remaining amount can be distributed.

When a house has a mortgage this fact is noted on a charge certificate which shows all relevant title details, including who the current registered owner is. The paper certifies that the building society has the house as security for the money it has loaned. Once the mortgage has been paid off the certificate is released.

Upon request, the building society will let you know the amount outstanding on the mortgage. Once the sale has been completed and the mortgage repaid, the society releases the charge certificate. On receipt of this certificate – sent on a special Land Registry form – it should be sent to the Land Registry who will cross out the details of the mortgage and return the land certificate – as it is now called – to the executor. This is formal proof that ownership of the house is free from any loan commitments.

Land Registry notes all property transactions throughout the United Kingdom. As executor, once probate has been given, you have to notify the Land Registry (offices in most towns and large cities, see telephone directory for the one nearest you) that the title of the property is now transferred to the ownership of the executors, in other words the estate. The house can be transferred directly to one of the beneficiaries but a further application – on the same form – has to be sent off to the Registry. Instead of the mortgage showing the names of the executors the name of the ultimate beneficiary has to be inserted.

The Land Registry form can be obtained by asking for Form 56 Assent or Approbation from either the Land Registry office nearest to you or from most bookshops. If using the services of a solicitor then this process will be undertaken on your behalf.

You should note on the form the title number, the address of the property concerned, the date, the names of the executors (and their addresses) as well as the name and address of the deceased. The form must be witnessed, with the witness supplying his full address and occupation.

LAND REGISTRY FEES
The Land Registry charges a fee based on the value of the house, whether the house has been transferred to a beneficiary or bought outright. The fee starts at £50 for a house valued at £40,000 and goes up to £200 for a house valued at £160,000 or over. If the house is not *full value*, in other words where there is not a sale, a separate scale known as 'A, Abatement 2' would apply. In this instance for a house valued at £40,000 the fee would be £25.

WHAT TO DO IF YOU CANNOT FIND A TITLE DEED
If you are unable to locate a title deed or a mortgage certificate and you doubt whether the house is registered, you should go to the Land Registry where you should be able to inspect details pertaining to the property. Upon proof of your role as executor, the Land Registry would be able to send a replacement of the lost title deed. As a rule of thumb, however, if there is no loan certificate or charge certificate then the title is not registered. This is still possible as compulsory registration has only been

introduced relatively recently. Indeed, in certain areas it means that some houses which have not been sold have not been registered.

Among the deceased's papers there may be a copy of the original conveyance sent to him by the solicitor at the time the house was purchased. This conveyance was the official document transferring ownership from the previous owner to the deceased. In the case of leasehold property the conveyance is called an assignment.

TRANSFERRING OWNERSHIP

Once you have this deed, you are able to prepare a document transferring ownership, whether as instructed in the will or as administrator in the case of intestacy. Again, as with the normal transfer of a registered property, the building society will give back the title deed to the property once the mortgage has been repaid. Attached to the mortgage deed will be an acknowledgement stating that the money has been paid off and the mortgage discharged. This deed will also include a copy of the deed of conveyance when the house was originally purchased by the deceased.

In order to make up an assent, the title deeds must accompany the deed of conveyance along with the original copy of the grant of probate. On the assent form you need to show the full details pertaining to the property, ie full address, the name and full address of the person to whom the property is being transferred. When returned to you, the forms are said to be 'assented', legal proof that the person died, the date of death and the date that probate was granted. This assent form should always be kept with the title deeds to the property.

A house held in joint ownership, held as joint tenants passing by survivorship, is more straightforward and no assent should be needed. A death certificate as proof that the survivor is now entitled to the property along with the deeds should be sufficient. However, if you are the beneficiary yourself you are, in effect, writing an assent to yourself. If you are representing a number of people then an assent form should be used.

LEASEHOLD PROPERTY

The 'landlord' or leaseholder of leasehold property has to be notified that an assent is being done and may charge a fee but this depends on the terms of the lease. He may also be entitled to retain a copy of the assent. On the form all details of the lease have to be noted, such as its length, what costs are attributed to it, etc.

Leasehold property starts its life usually with 99 years noted on the title deeds. As time marches on so the lease's expiry date comes closer to completion. When this occurs the property reverts back to the owner (or landlord) of the lease, but until that time you own the leasehold property and can sell it on. However, the owner of the freehold on the property has to be informed of any lease transfer taking place. The same form for the transfer of ownership of freehold property is used.

When the beneficiary eventually comes to sell the house the original grant of probate, along with assent, may need to be shown to prove legal ownership.

Because these property transfers can be fraught with danger when the beneficiary comes to sell – especially if the property is unregistered – it would be best to approach a solicitor and ask him to deal with matters. Instances have occurred when, at the final stage of selling a house, the purchaser's solicitor has noted that the property had not been legally transferred and the sale has been halted.

Bookkeeping

As an executor, it is your duty to keep a careful record of all amounts of money, property and any outstanding debts. This naturally necessitates bookkeeping.

You should keep a ledger noting all the amounts of money paid out, such as funeral expenses, telephone calls, train fares, petrol, stationery, even down to the last 19p stamp. Keep a receipt for each item of expenditure and cross reference this receipt with the same number noted in the ledger. Assets that have been sold in preparation for distribution should be noted on a separate page, stating when and where they were sold, the amount received for each item and where the money now is.

Money could be held on deposit and if so, any interest payments received must also be included.

Dividend payments should also be noted along with any shares or other investments that have subsequently been sold. All of these will have vouchers which must be kept safely and again cross-referenced to the ledger.

Any tax that has been deducted from dividends or interest payments must be noted on your ledger, as eventually a repayment situation could arise. Interestingly, although an investment tax on gains made on share transactions, known as stamp duty, is payable, provided the beneficiary of the shares is also an executor of the will, a letter of bequest can be granted with the result that there is no stamp duty to pay.

It cannot be stressed too often that accurate and detailed books need to be kept. As an executor you can be asked up to 12 years after the date your duty first commenced to show what payments were received and what distributions were made. If you keep accurate accounts then it is unlikely that any charge of maladministration can be levied against you.

It is a good idea to keep back a certain amount of money in case further payments need to be made but more importantly, it keeps the estate liquid. There is a further example of the benefit in doing this. Suppose there is an existing business and the expenses of that business are higher than the interest being received. If there is no liquidity then certain assets may have to be sold and the best possible price not obtained. Another example is that a beneficiary might need payment before final distribution takes place or perhaps creditors may need an interim or complete payment.

By keeping accurate accounts you can quickly pull together all the transactions once completion has taken place and the final winding-up procedure account-wise will be relatively simple.

Tax returns

As executor of the estate you are responsible for completing income tax returns on the estate's behalf. As there is no individual concerned then no personal tax relief is granted. For income tax purposes, the only relief that an estate can claim back is if it has had to obtain a loan from a bank in order to pay inheritance tax or the probate fee (using form R59).

Before distribution, you have to fill in an income tax return form showing your assessment of how much tax is due based on the income received. This form is then duly signed and returned to the Revenue, who, if they agree with it, send you a demand for the estate tax due. Once this tax has been paid distribution can take place. Always ask the Revenue for a receipt of any tax paid as proof of the discharge of the estate's income tax liability.

When completing the income tax form (R1) you need to insert the period of administration. Hopefully, the winding up procedure will not take longer than a year but for each new year it enters a new income tax return form must be filled in.

Any shares or unit trusts which have been sold must be included on this form and shown in the following order.

1. Number of shares sold.
2. Value of shares (in other words how much did you receive from the sale?).
3. The date of the sale.
4. Any commissions or costs that were incurred.

This procedure has to be followed for each set of company shares sold. At the bottom of each entry you have to insert what money was made. You should insert what price the shares were bought at, less the price they were sold at less commission charges and stamp duty.

If the shares have risen in value then you have to show the gain. Alongside the details write the phrase 'exempt £5000' which refers to the amount of annual allowable capital gain before tax. Any loss that has been made can be set off against any other capital gain that the estate might have made.

Once the tax forms have been filled in they should be returned to the Inland Revenue, along with a letter formally giving notice that the administration of the estate has been closed, and giving the exact date when the completion of the estate occurred. Any tax credits due from dividends must be included and reimbursement asked for. As there may be residuary beneficiaries of the will you can ask for a tax form, R185E, to be sent to you on their behalf. One form per person is needed. Remember to ask for confirmation that the Revenue have closed the estate's file and ask that any dividend folios sent are returned, as you will need these as evidence when preparing the final distribution.

The forms should then be returned to you together with any repayment. But it is one thing to owe the Revenue money and quite another to collect it. The Revenue ask you to pay within 30 days.

Accounts

After gaining probate, all assets and liabilities can be settled and on doing this the estate is considered to be complete. The legacies can now be distributed.

Should you have incurred expenses as executor you will now be able to reimburse yourself out of the executorship bank account. If the will states that executors should be paid then their account can also be settled.

All the beneficiaries should now receive a letter from you stating that the estate is ready for distribution and that their legacy can be collected.

Distributing legacies

As an executor you are responsible for ensuring that there are no loose ends. Therefore, each legacy that is handed over to the beneficiary must be signed for. The receipt should contain the following information:

(a) details of the sum of money or description of the legacy;
(b) full details of the estate's executors;
(c) who the gift was given to under the terms of the deceased's will;
(d) signed by the person who received the legacy.

A copy of this receipt should be kept for your records and the other copy retained by the beneficiary.

A slight problem does arise if a beneficiary is under the age of 18. Legally a child cannot sign a receipt. In order to overcome this problem, the father or mother or lawful guardian should sign on the child's behalf with the proviso that when he reaches the age of majority he will receive the money or gift plus any interest earned.

It is worth noting that a child under the age of 18 can also receive an income tax allowance as a single person. So it is not tax efficient for any sums of money to be placed in savings accounts where tax is deducted at source unless the interest earned in a year is likely to exceed £2785 (current rate). Banks and building societies now automatically deduct basic rate tax from monies held with them and it is not recoverable. Instead, you should open an account where money is paid gross and not net, for example with National Savings accounts.

Once all the pecuniary legacies have been paid, the executor can re-examine whether any creditors have been overlooked or, for that matter, anything of relevance to the estate. The time should be used for double-checking that everything that should have been done has been done. Once you are happy that this is the case then final accounts can be prepared.

Final accounts

If the bookkeeping has been done accurately it will be a

straightforward matter to pull all the accounts together. Each sheet of accounts should be clearly headed, noting the period of administration, the deceased person's name and the type of account to be found on the sheet.

CAPITAL ACCOUNTS

The first and prime account sheet is the capital account. On one side this shows what the assets value were on the date of death, eg property less outstanding mortgage, the value of any life insurance policies, pension premiums, building society or bank accounts, National Savings, shares, retirement pensions and so on. It itemises all assets and their value and then any debts, noted on the other side of the sheet, are deducted from this amount. Debts include probate fees, inheritance tax, bank charges, Land Registry fee and so on.

Looking at the last bank statement, you should see if the amount agrees with the total amount shown in your calculations. If so, this is the final and true account. If not then you must go over the accounts again until they are reconciled.

INCOME ACCOUNT

The income account is the next sheet that needs to be completed. It should include any income received throughout the period of administration. In other words, any dividends that have been paid, any profits paid on the trust, any interest paid on the bank account etc, less the amount of tax deducted at source. Not only are receipts shown in the income account but also any payments that have been made, for example mortgage repayment. The final figure shown should match exactly the final figure given on the income tax return form.

To be included on the income account sheet is any tax repayment to the estate.

DISTRIBUTIONS SHEET

The last sheet to be completed is the distribution sheet. Again, all details pertaining to the estate need to be noted.

Capital Accounts – Example

Estate accounts covering the period of administration from date of death 10 October 1988 to 5 April 1989.

Receipts

	£	£
Somerset Farm	75,000	75,000
Broadwood (half of value)	100,000	50,000
Contents		2,500
Antiques		4,900
Jewellery		1,650
National Savings Certificates		5,000
Building society account (1)		3,000
Building society account (2)		2,000
Premium Bonds		500
Life insurance policy		20,000
Endowment policy (with profits)		10,500
Stocks and shares (see separate list)		15,000
Cash		100
Interest paid on building society accounts		150
Gain on shares sold		900
Interest on National Savings		100
		191,300

Less Payments		
Half of mortgage		20,000
Funeral account		1,250
Probate fee		150
Inheritance tax		24,020
Bank charges		35
Executor's expenses		145
Debts outstanding at death		1,000
Legacies paid		1,000
Debts paid from the estate		47,600
Balance of estate to distribution account		143,700

(Note £1,000 of legacy has already been paid)

Signatures:

Executor .... Approved by ....

Date ....

Note: The figures shown are approximations.

At the top of the sheet insert the remaining amount of money still held by the estate. This figure will be found in the capital account sheet. All payments made out to the beneficiaries need to be itemised even if they include a house and contents, shares or unit trusts or the residue in the bank account. Each beneficiary in receipt of a legacy must have his name and what he is receiving noted here and its value. The total figure should match exactly with the receipts brought across from the capital and income sheets.

The closing stages

It is recommended that the distribution of the estate, unless it is a small and uncomplicated one, should not be completed under a six-month period. This is because under inheritance tax a claimant can come forward up to six months from the date probate was granted. There are special circumstances where the time limit may be extended by the court.

If the estate has already been distributed then the executors could be looking at a court case whereby the claimant can state that he was not treated equally or his claim was not considered when it should have been.

Once all the accounts have been written up the beneficiaries are entitled to have the opportunity to study them, if they so wish. They might have certain questions regarding the distribution, tax or interest payment – all need to be answered. When each beneficiary has seen the accounts and agreed them, each person must sign the bottom of all account sheets.

Once cheques have been given to the beneficiaries and your receipts filed safely away, write to the bank advising that all payments have been made and that the executorship account should now be closed. Usually banks charge fees for handling administrative work. This fee will be deducted from the money held in the account. Whatever money is left is given to the residuary beneficiary.

All papers together with the signed copy of the account should be placed in a safe place along with the probate certificates.

Appendices

APPENDIX 1

PROBATE CHECKLIST

1. Register death and obtain death certificate (additional copies if necessary) from the nearest Registrar of Births, Deaths and Marriages.
2. If the deceased left instructions for organ donation make sure that this request is passed on to the medical staff.
3. If directed under the will, consider funeral arrangements.
4. Collect the will. Obtain photocopies. If the deceased died intestate consider whether you want to apply to administer the estate. If so obtain the necessary forms from the Personal Applications Department of the nearest Probate Registry.
5. Do you need a grant of probate for an existing will or letters of administration in the case of intestacy? Ask the Probate Registry to send you the forms.
6. Collect details of all assets and liabilities for valuation purposes. Write off to relevant institutions including banks confirming the death, your position and asking for a valuation up to the date of death and whether tax has been deducted. If the estate is insolvent see a solicitor immediately.
7. Prepare a valuation sheet for the approximate value of all items in the estate. Start bookkeeping ledgers.
8. If the deceased was a beneficiary under a trust or life interest, ask the relevant person what each trust or life interest is, including its value and terms and if necessary seek legal advice.
9. Start to collect all assets. Fill in forms.
10. Return all forms to the Probate Registry along with the death certificate.
11. Confirm date of appointment given to you by the Probate Registry.
12. Arrange finance if necessary to pay for inheritance tax, probate fees.
13. Attend Probate Registry, swear forms, pay probate fee, if necessary pay inheritance tax.

14. Receive grant of probate or letters of administration.
15. If necessary, put a statutory advertisement in local or national papers asking for creditors and other claimants against the estate to reply. Seek legal advice if necessary.
16. If property has been valued by the valuation officer from the Inland Revenue agree the declared value. Additional inheritance tax might have to be paid.
17. Complete income tax forms and capital gains tax for the period of administration.
18. Apply for and get inheritance tax discharge certificate.
19. Either through loan or through available cash in the estate, pay off any estate liabilities.
20. Pay and transfer any legacies, obtaining receipts.
21. Prepare the final estate accounts with the appropriate tax deduction certificate, R185E.
22. If the will provides for life interests or trusts seek legal advice, as the part of the estate allocated to this will now need transferring over to the trustees.
23. Obtain approval of accounts and receipts from beneficiaries.
24. Distribute assets to beneficiaries or residuary beneficiary.
25. Write to the bank closing the bank account.

PROBATE FEES PAYABLE BY A PERSONAL APPLICANT IN ENGLAND AND WALES

Net estate £	Fee £
0 – 500	1.00
501 – 1,000	2.00
1,001 – 5,000	5.00
5,001 – 6,000	6.00
6,001 – 7,000	7.00
7,001 – 8,000	8.00
8,001 – 9,000	9.00
9,001 – 10,000	10.00
10,001 – 25,000	£40.00 plus £1.00 for every £1,000 or part of £1,000
25,001 – 40,000	£80.00 plus £1.00 for every £1,000 or part of £1,000
40,001 – 100,000	£3.50 for every £1,000 or part of £1,000
Over £100,000	£250.00 for the first £100,000 and £50.00 for every additional £100,000 or part of £100,000 Plus £1.00 for every £1,000 or part of £1,000

Source: HMSO PA4

PERSONAL FINANCE TITLES FROM KOGAN PAGE

Blackstone Franks Good Investment Guide, The, David Franks, 1987
Buying and Selling a House or Flat, Howard and Jackie Green, 1988
Cashwise: How to Achieve More from a Fixed Income, Frank Birkin, 1987
Easing into Retirement, Keith Hughes, 1987
How to Write a Will and Gain Probate, Marlene Garsia, 1989
Living and Retiring Abroad, 3rd edn, Michael Furnell, 1989
Making Money from Penny Shares and Small Company Investments, Adrian
 Ball, 1989
Managing Your Money, Anthea Masey, 1988
Personal Pensions: The Choice is Yours, Norman Toulson, 1987

INDEX

ST